Tracks in the
Psychic Wilderness

Tracks in the Psychic Wilderness

An Exploration of Remote Viewing, ESP, Precognitive Dreaming, and Synchronicity

By the Former Director of Stargate

Dale E. Graff

with a Foreword by Dr. Edgar Mitchell

ELEMENT

Boston, Massachusetts
Shaftesbury, Dorset
Melbourne, Victoria

First published in the USA in 1998 by
Element Books, Inc.
160 North Washington Street, Boston, MA 02114

Published in Great Britain in 1998 by
Element Books Limited
Shaftesbury, Dorset SP7 8BP

Published in Australia in 1998 by
Element Books Limited
and distributed by Penguin Australia Limited
487 Maroondah Highway, Ringwood, Victoria 3134

Reprinted 1998

Designed by Vernon Press, Inc., Boston, MA
Printed and bound in the United States by Courier Westford, Inc., Westford, MA

Library of Congress Cataloging-in-Publication Data

Graff, Dale E.
    Tracks in the psychic wilderness : an exploration of ESP, remote
viewing, precognitive dreaming, and synchronicity / Dale E. Graff. —
1st ed.
        p.   cm.
    Includes bibliographical references.
    ISBN 1-86204-203-9 (hardcover : alk. paper)
    1. Parapsychology.   I. Title.
BF1031.G58   1998
133.8—dc21   97-39391
                                                    CIP

British Library Cataloguing-in-Publication data available.

First Edition
ISBN 1-86204-203-9

Dedication

To Barbara, my wife, who has enjoyed our travels in the Canadian wilds and has shared my inner-wilderness journeys.

To my children, Diane and Dale, Jr., who share the spirit of exploration.

There's no sense in going further, "it's the edge of cultivation,"
So they said, and I believed it...
Till a voice, as bad as Conscience, rang interminable changes
On one everlasting Whisper day and night repeated—so:
"Something hidden. Go and find it. Go and look behind the Ranges."
    "The Explorer"
    —Rudyard Kipling

Contents

Developing Your psi Potential   159

Foreword

Dr. Edgar Mitchell

Former U.S. astronaut and
author of *The Way of the Explorer*

It is now reasonably certain that, even before the historical period, humans as well as nonhuman species had an internal intuitive, or "visceral," knowing, which has been called a "sixth sense." It now seems that it should have been called the "first sense" because modern research leads us to believe that it is based upon a complex form of quantum correlation that was certainly present in nature long before species evolved to their current stage, and even before the planetary environment evolved to produce the normal five senses. Research in a frontier field called the quantum hologram leads us to that conclusion. It helps to explain virtually all the "non-local" intuitive, psychic, and numinous effects that humans have reported during historic times but have previously been unable to understand in terms of this world's natural processes.

Due in large measure to the seventeenth-century Cartesian dogma of dualism, which pronounced mind and body as being different stuff, classical Western science soon began to discount remote internal sensing of any kind. The result has been that folk of all walks of life, particularly the brightest and most gifted, had to hide their intuitive and deep psychic abilities for fear of being labeled a witch in earlier years, or being ostracized in some fashion even in modern times. For those who have spent many years compiling scientific data on intuitive (psychic) functioning—data that in any other field of science would be considered overwhelming—it will be most gratifying to know that a simple physical, informational structure called the quantum hologram, which is associated with the nonlocal wave characteristics of every physical object, is likely the proper explanation for their data. Although quantum physics is itself almost ethereal and mystical, it is a well-established understanding of nature and has allowed scientists to probe human experience previously unreachable.

The brave pioneers in the sciences who dared challenge Cartesian dogma have finally produced the evidence, both with theory and experiment, to demonstrate that information, emotions, and even physical effects can be shared by resonance with a nonlocal object. Dale Graff is one of those pioneers who risked a career and "respectability" to pursue the truth. It is wonderful that he writes his story as there are many such stories to be told, but until the current moment in modern history, it was enormously risky to do so.

Preface

In this book, I discuss an as-yet unexplained mental ability to access information without using our physical senses (e.g., sight, taste, hearing, etc.). Some instances of intuition are probably due to this type of knowing. Such terms as extrasensory perception (ESP), telepathy, clairvoyance, and precognition have been used to identify this unexplained ability.

"Remote viewing," a more recent descriptor for this phenomenon, is gaining wider use by researchers and practitioners. Information perceived during a remote viewing experience is usually visual; that is, "sights" such as scenes or buildings at a specific geographic site are perceived. However, other types of sensory information can also become known. Some remote reviewing practitioners include specific techniques in their definition of remote viewing. I consider remote viewing to be an unknown process similar to ESP that is independent of the manner in which it is approached.

I also include experiences of synchronicity in this book, since I believe the roots of synchronicity are linked to phenomena like ESP. Synchronicity refers to events that appear to be unusual coincidences, but have significance and meaning that other coincidences lack.

Some people have an ability to cause apparent interactions with matter—moving objects or affecting electronic devices, for example—by mental intention alone. This phenomenon appears to be energetic and is referred to as psychokinesis, which means "mind-motion." Some researchers suspect that psychokinesis is related to precognition. Those who research these informational and energetic mental phenomenon are known as parapsychologists.

In the 1940s, B. P. Wiesner and R. L. Thouless, researchers at the Society for Psychical Research in England, began use of the twenty-third letter of the Greek alphabet—*psi* (pronounced like "sigh")—to represent these informational and energetic phenomena. This neutral label avoided implications of how these phenomena function. Older terms, such as telepathy, implied that a type of radiation was responsible, which psi does not. This new neutral term also helped to minimize associations with sensationalistic media interpretations of this phenomena.

I prefer to use psi as a general reference for these unexplained mental capacities and I cite it frequently in this book. Some people are more familiar with the term *psychic phenomena,* which includes psi. However, psychic phenomena can also entail a variety of other experiences that have a wide range of subjective interpretations.

In the end, however, the specific terms we use to describe psi phenomena are not important. What matters is how psi can be of help to ourselves and to others, and what psi can add to our understanding of ourselves and the nature of the universe.

My approach to any new venture is that of an explorer: search, find, examine, evaluate; follow the paths of others when necessary, search for new tracks whenever possible. If there is no trail, I then search for tracks that lead to one, no matter what the nature of the wilderness may be. Important discoveries result from motivated searching.

When I find something, I then ask, What is it? What does it mean? How can it improve understanding of the world into which we are born? What can these discoveries do for myself and others?

Early interest in wilderness exploration led me to frontiers in engineering and science—designing space vehicles, tracking satellites, following scientific activities of other countries. In the early 1970s, when I first encountered the world of psi and our inner domain, I knew this was the vast frontier that I had unknowingly been looking for.

Over the past three decades I have been directly involved in psi research, both professionally and personally. Official responsibilities emphasized remote viewing phenomenon, while personal explorations have taken me into all aspects of psi.

My first exposure to any wilderness was as a tracker of animals. I discovered the subtle ways of animals, their elusive nature, how difficult they were to follow. I learned the secrets of tracks and what they revealed of the track makers. I began exploring the psi domain like a tracker searching to see if anything was there. When I found tracks, I looked at them from different angles, seeking their significance.

In time, the tracks of psi I came upon were clearly visible. They were on a trail that I and others could see. Encouraged by early successes, I continued exploring. I am now reexamining those tracks. Writing about them enhances my understanding; it may also help others in some way.

Tracks in the Psychic Wilderness includes vignettes of a few of my trackings, presented in the context in which they occurred. Any experience needs a context for its meaning to unfold. These are episodes I directly observed or experienced; they are what I know best. They helped me move, unafraid, a few steps further along the trail. Once I found them, they were easy to rediscover, especially in times of need.

To some people my vignettes may resemble "only experiments," or only "this or that." To me, they are exceptional experiences. They provided a beginning understanding of myself, they let me know the deeper feelings of others, and they showed me how we are all interconnected.

The years ahead will have many twists and turns on the path toward our understanding of this vast frontier—our inner wilderness; our psi domain. There, new paths and tracks can be found. We need to look for those that resonate within us and follow those trails. Intersections will occur; we will learn that we are all going in the same direction.

Anyone with a balanced approach, a caring attitude, and motivation can search for psi tracks.

Stargate—A Personal View

That November night in 1995 I gazed at Ted Koppel's "Nightline" television program in disbelief. There it was in plain view: the story on Stargate, the United States government's innovative program for research into applications of remote viewing, an aspect of extrasensory perception. The psychic part of the Cold War was over; Project Stargate had been discontinued. That is, the official part of Stargate was over. What about the people who came into the program? Why did they—why did I—risk our careers to chase after remote viewing rainbows? That part of Stargate would never be over.

"Nightline" closed one door and opened another. Our individual stories could now be told; we could now continue exploring remote viewing and other aspects of psi in the open. No more locked doors, no more compartments within compartments. The falling of the Iron Curtain, the tearing down of the Berlin Wall cracked many barriers within both Russia and the U.S., and Stargate had been concealed by one of them.

But there was another reason for my disbelief, even shock, at that ABC "Nightline" program: I was on it!

Of course I knew I would be. A week earlier I had been interviewed by Dr. Michael Guillen, the ABC Science Editor, and I knew that a portion of that interview would make it into the program. As I watched myself on TV, it was difficult to accept the fact that I was on the program, and that Stargate was now becoming common knowledge. But there it was, on that far-reaching screen, after twenty years.

I clicked off the TV when "Nightline" signed off. Outside, the Chesapeake Bay heaved wind-blown waves against the cliff. Stars sent faint light from a cosmic distance. They may forever remain out of reach, but not the Stargate within. Our inner Stargate can be found by anyone who chooses to search.

The time had come to reflect over what had been, what could have been, and what could come next. In pursuing our dream of advancing a new frontier, had we caught something of value?

I knew I had to begin writing about the experiences that showed me the reality of our psi potential. Through them, psi became real. They gave me the insights that motivated me to guide Stargate's research and applications and illustrated how psi phenomena can be applied both for my own use and for helping others. My experiences validated what my intuition had always known. Now I understood what others had been describing for centuries.

I discovered that by exploring our psychic realm, we automatically become more creative and intuitive. We sense deeper aspects of our psyche and discover how our minds can reach beyond physical limits. As we uncover our psychic talents, we are able to help others in ways that would not be possible otherwise.

I wrote *Tracks in the Psychic Wilderness* to describe personal observations and interactions that illustrate some of the psi events we can all experience: remote viewing, ESP, psychic dreams, and synchronicity. They helped me begin Stargate explorations and overcome the many storms that blew my way. They gave me the confidence to withstand the criticism, the skeptics, and the discouragements.

What was Stargate? How had it begun? What role had I played in the Stargate adventure?

In 1975, I was diligently pursuing a career in aerospace engineering and physics with the Air Force's Foreign Technology Division (FTD), in Dayton, Ohio. Among my responsibilities was the analysis of technical sensor data from optics, radar, and other electronic devices. I wrote assessment reports on emerging technologies, including forecasts to the year 2000 and beyond. Little did I anticipate then that one of my forecasts would radically change my life. It would place my career in jeopardy; it would take me away from the safety of a conventional profession. But it would also bring me into contact with a new perspective on reality and show me that I and others possess unsuspected abilities.

As I wrote that technology-forecast paper, I came to realize the difficulty of accurately predicting anything more than a few years ahead—let alone twenty or thirty! Technology trends alone were insufficient. The political, economic, or sociological factors could shift possible futures at any moment. What about the human element, the stroke of genius, the breakthrough, and the psychological aspects, including parapsychology, the science that studies psychic phenomena such as ESP?

If at least some aspects of psychic phenomena are real, then why should they not be explored? And how can this phenomena be used? Were other countries ahead of us in this field? In quiet moments I sometimes wondered about my own unusual experiences. I suspected some of them were not totally due to chance.

I ignored our organizational constraints and added a section on other considerations, including parapsychology. To make a case for the existence of these phenomena—or psi—I summarized results from the best research I could find, which included Soviet work on ESP and telepathy that had been published in technical journals from the U.S.S.R. Their reports hinted at telepathic-communication experiments with submarines and the "transmission of emotion" over intercontinental distances. Some of their cosmonauts were interested in ESP.

I had some trepidation about including this topic. Would it cast me as a "fuzzy thinker"—the charge made by many psychologists and others who take strong negative views toward these phenomena? However, research evidence supported its existence. I had heard accounts of psychic events from credible people and the Soviets had shown an interest in psi applications.

To my surprise, Command Level at FTD liked the futuristic cast of my paper and its broad view. The psi research that existed, especially the Soviet work, surprised them. They asked me to keep an eye on this field and let them know what else I might uncover.

I thought that would be the end of it—a show of interest, then back to business as usual. But I had opened a door…certainly an unusual one in my practical scientific environment. A few months later, I received an unexpected invitation from the chief scientist to attend a briefing. The topic: remote viewing.

Dr. Harold Puthoff and Russell Targ, physicists at the Stanford Research Institute (SRI), had contacted our organization to explain their remote viewing research. My forecast paper had been the key for accepting the SRI visit request. Hal and Russ were looking for funding to continue their remote viewing activities, which had started in 1972. In their briefing, Hal and Russ showed us data that could not be written off to chance. A few of the operational projects included sites in the Soviet Union. Remote viewing of a Soviet nuclear test facility had details that were later verified by satellite photography. But their main funding source, the Central Intelligence Agency (CIA), had withdrawn support for political reasons.

After the briefing, I was called into a closed session with our chief scientist and a few command staff personnel. Should our organization keep the research alive, or let it dry up? Hal and Russ were about to return to conventional research.

If remote viewing was real, we could anticipate several interesting applications—locating missing airplanes and pilots, prisoners of war and hostages. If people with remote viewing ability could describe areas behind the Iron Curtain accurately enough, they could alert us to new developments. Remote viewing could help us avoid technological surprise. We already used many conventional techniques devoted to that goal, including data from aircraft and satellites, radar tracking, and clandestine travelers.

A few days after that meeting, I met again with the chief scientist. FTD Command had agreed to support the SRI remote viewing research for at least one year to see what was there, to keep a step ahead, to avoid surprise. I became the contract manager.

That is how I helped initiate remote viewing research in the Department of Defense (DOD), and how I began my new career. I quickly identified our remote viewing research interests and launched into the new enterprise.

Our research considered two basic questions: (1) Is there a physical basis, perhaps in quantum physics, that would help in understanding remote viewing and its operating parameters? and (2) How accurate and reliable could remote viewing data be? We knew that insight into these questions would clarify what types of applications were the most feasible as well as how to accomplish them. We also wanted to replicate the Soviet ESP work to evaluate their claims.

Results from our first year's contractual effort had reasonable success, and we extended our research for several years. Eventually, other DOD agencies became interested in the SRI research, and small review groups were formed. Due to the controversial nature of the topic, only personnel at appropriate command, review, and analytical areas were informed. We chose those with a balanced point of view who could critically review the research but remain open-minded. People with either strong negative feelings or who too readily accepted the phenomenon would have made it difficult to accomplish unbiased examination of remote viewing activities.

We achieved sufficient success to warrant continued remote viewing research. Our findings, along with earlier SRI work, motivated an Army-intelligence organization to consider setting up an in-house remote viewing unit at Fort Meade, Maryland. I was called in to explain our replications of the SRI work and to present the Soviet ESP data. That information helped the Army establish their project.

Shortly after I began my role as manager for the remote viewing research contract with SRI, I found people within FTD who had remote viewing talent and could replicate the SRI findings. Our successes became known and we were brought into operational projects to see if our remote viewing data could help search teams locate missing airplanes. When the results from one of those search projects proved to be very accurate, our data was leaked to the media, unfortunately. Antagonistic articles quickly appeared in national newspapers and other articles soon followed that sensationalized the potential of remote viewing. High-level Air Force management responded to this unwanted publicity by discontinuing our remote viewing investigations at FTD.

In order to continue remote viewing exploration, I accepted a position as a physicist with the Defense Intelligence Agency (DIA) in Washington, D.C. I helped reestablish research ties with SRI and set up links with the Army in-house remote viewing team, which was focused solely on operational applications. In 1985 this unit was transferred to the DIA for consolidation and several years later I joined them as their director. I continued managing external remote viewing research and writing reviews of Soviet ESP research activity. For the first time all aspects of remote viewing were brought together as a single integrated effort.

Having initiated DOD remote viewing research over a decade earlier, I was now the director of all DOD remote viewing activity—both research and applications. Our application projects included the Customs Department, Drug Enforcement Agency, Secret Service, and a variety of intelligence organizations.

As part of my responsibilities, I created the name "Stargate" for our total remote viewing effort. Stargate invoked the feeling of exploration, a sense of reaching beyond our ordinary capabilities, of expanding the boundaries of our human potential. Other terms, such as "Grill Flame" and "Sun Streak," had been used for earlier government remote viewing activity, but Stargate caught our imagination as an appropriate name for this innovative program. It will always symbolize the project and the potential within each of us.

After Ted Koppel signed off, I paced around, wondering. Many times over the past two decades I tried to rationalize why I had accepted that early remote viewing research role at FTD. I may never know if my innate sense of exploration, my need to find out what lies behind the range, is so strong that I risked my profession, but I did discover, or *un*cover, a hidden dimension within myself and others. Something was there. There were discernable tracks in that psychic wilderness.

Many of those with whom I worked were also driven by the need to explore, to know, and to help others in some way—search and rescue, avoid surprise, be forewarned. I believe the need to avoid surprise is part of our survival instinct. Our psychic nature lurks below the surface of consciousness, ever ready to help us live more efficiently, if not consciously then, where possible, through unconscious actions, those sudden hunches and intuitions.

Stargate certainly changed the lives of my remote viewing colleagues, too. Most responded well to the challenges. Unfortunately, a few saw it as an opportunity for commercial gain and have been making unrealistic claims. They were not ready for this field. There is the issue of physical–mental balance. As in anything, we can easily go to extremes if we do not remain connected with our rational nature and physical world. No one can be totally rational; no one can be totally intuitive or psychic. We encouraged a solid exercise regime for physical and psychological well-being. We explored the phenomenon from a natural, neutral perspective.

How did we locate remote viewers? Since we could not openly advertise for them, at times we relied on word of mouth. Those who were interested simply demonstrated what they could do in an experimental situation. If they did well, they were considered. Early in the project's life, we applied insights from the Myers Briggs Test Inventory (MBTI), which provides a way of profiling personality types. We found that people who did well on the intuition, feeling, and perception measures were likely to do well in remote viewing, though not always. Usually people who were curious, open-minded, and spontaneous did well. Some parapsychology researchers have found that people who have frequent childhood experiences of a psychic nature are the best candidates. Although we found many people who had good remote viewing potential, not many wanted to pursue it as career since it presented too many professional risks.

Because remote viewing does not involve a deep altered state, a remote viewer is alert and awake during a session. Perceptions—usually images, and sometimes sensations or feelings—manifest themselves in a daydreamlike condition. A degree of relaxation is needed, but not as deep as those described for some meditation states.

In order to begin a remote viewing session, individuals follow different approaches to reach a relaxed state. Some listen to soft music, some to loud rock. Others walk around, work idly on a calming activity, or sit quietly in order to minimize routine thinking. During this "cool-down" phase, they occasionally affirm their desire and willingness to receive viewing impressions.

Remote viewers tended to have varying project preferences. Some did well describing remote scenes, including structural information that might be present. Some were better at sensing movement or changes at the target areas. Others excelled in identifying sensations and feelings associated with the target. These preferences related to cognitive style and personality, and had to be considered in project assignment or in how the data were evaluated.

The data generated by a remote viewer during a session was highly variable. Sometimes there was little or no correlation with the intended target; at other times, a high degree of accuracy was achieved. High motivation and the greater importance of a project usually generated more accurate results. We also discovered that the attitudes of those in management positions had a clear affect on performance, as they would for any creative activity. Remote viewers are susceptible to ill winds, even if subtle, they pick up from others.

As has been observed in research laboratories, when attitudes are positive and encouraging, remote viewers are enthusiastic and perform well. Some researchers do not achieve consistent results; those with good interpersonal skills or a strong desire for success do.

Remote viewing activity should be as distraction- and noise-free as possible. The isolation of our two small barracks buildings at Fort Meade provided for that. The rooms used for remote viewing sessions had plain acoustical tile on the walls and ceiling to reduce external noise and distractions. Occasionally low-flying helicopters, screeching ambulance sirens, or cannon shots during a nearby a military ceremony jarred the silence of a remote viewing session. Even though the peeled-paint exterior looked awful, regardless of appearances, we all preferred this setting.

Oh, the thoughts that raced through my mind that night after "Nightline." Yes. We had achieved something of value. We knew remote viewing impressions have a mix of error and correct data, as does any sensor. It also has potentially useful information. We were like prospectors, extracting gold from a dusky place.

Many of the early Stargate projects examined remote viewing for alerts and tip-offs to technical developments in the Soviet Union. To gain insight into the tip-off potential, we asked remote viewers to describe technical areas in the United States, which we could then compare to known information. We called these projects "simulation" or "calibration" exercises.

Based on the results, we were able to determine how well a remote viewer might do when asked to describe technical sites in the Soviet Union. The only information given to the remote viewer was an abstract-target identifier, such as an Earth coordinate. Since Earth coordinates could provide a general idea of geographic features, we considered only structures or manmade configurations—information not available from any map—in our evaluation. Later, only abstract labels, such as "Project X," were used.

A few of the early calibration projects were for technical areas in the San Francisco Bay area—for example, a laser-development facility or a high energy–particle accelerator. Results were very good, indicating that remote viewing could be used to describe technical facilities. A series of remote viewing calibration projects involving equipment was also successful.

The goal of one early calibration project was the description of the general features of the Strategic Command Headquarters in Omaha, Nebraska. The viewer, who was in Menlo Park, California, had no prior knowledge of the area. The sketches produced closely resembled the layout of the target site, including missiles displayed near the entrance. In an evaluation project, remote viewers were asked to describe a rocket-motor test site in a western-American desert. Their main objective was to see if they could detect when a test firing occurred. The first few rocket tests were delayed due to equipment malfunction. At those times, the remote viewers sensed nothing energetic. However, when the rocket test actually fired, the two remote viewers sensed the occurrence of an energetic, explosionlike event within several seconds of the actual firing. One of the remote viewers provided an accurate sketch of the actual test-stand layout—information that was not available from any map. Projects like these gave us confidence that remote viewing had tip-off potential regarding activity in Soviet military and technical-development areas.

Recent experiments continue to confirm the potential of remote viewing for determining accurate technical information at distant sites. In one experiment, a remote viewer one thousand miles away provided sketches that resembled the microwave generator at the target area in the New Mexico desert. His sketch illustrated how the device operated and was drawn to the proper scale. He also correctly perceived the general purpose of the device. Impressions included a technical area near the target site—a solar energy–collection facility. His perceptions of this facility included the presence of mirrorlike configurations that "catch something evenly."

In a similar project, he accurately described the external layout and technical details of a specific target at the Lawrence Livermore National Laboratory, thirty miles away in California. His sketches of a particle accelerator corresponded well with ground truth. For both these projects, he had been kept blind regarding the location of the target area. The only information he had was the name and photograph of the person visiting those sites, who could have been anywhere in the country.

An earlier remote viewing project, which took place during the brief CIA sponsorship of Stargate, was successful in describing specific details of a suspected Soviet nuclear-development facility at Semipalatinsk. The viewer, Pat Price, accurately drew a huge gantry. His sketches showed construction details of how high-energy explosions were contained; information that was not known at the time and was only confirmed later by satellite photographs. Pat described a large metal sphere, sixty feet in diameter, being assembled from thick metal gores that looked like sections of an orange peel. He perceived welding difficulty and the need for new material.* Three years later, the May 2, 1977, issue of *Aviation Week* reported that new, high-resolution satellite photography had detected thick steel segments for assembling a fifty-eight-foot sphere. This sphere was suspected to store energy from nuclear-driven explosives or pulse-power generators.

Around this time, Pat had provided accurate information on a classified communication site in West Virginia, including several project code words. He also perceived a similar site in the Ural Mountains, which was later confirmed. Pat was a former police officer who frequently had used his psi talent for locating suspects and solving crimes.

My first remote viewing–application project, which occurred in the late 1970s, while I was still at FTD, was to locate a missing Soviet airplane in a jungle region. I was the monitor and protocol developer for this search

---

*Data released per Freedom of Information Act.

project. No one had any knowledge of the specific search area. The only information provided to the remote viewers was the continent of the search and the type of aircraft. The remote viewers included one of the SRI people, Gary Langford, and Diane, a psi-talented individual I had discovered at FTD (see chapter 3, "Surprise at the Library").

Gary drew a detailed sketch of the perceived crash area. Diane, however, drew a sketch of the flight path and nearby landmarks. The search team confirmed that her sketches resembled features in the suspected forty-thousand-square-mile search zone. When given a topographic map of that region, Diane marked an area she believed to be the most likely spot, based on a match with her sketches. This was sent to the field team, who did not act on this information immediately since they believed the actual crash site to be over sixty miles away. One day later, a local inhabitant found the crash site. Diane's map marking was within three miles of where the plane actually was found.

Those of us who were directly involved were elated. We had come very close. Years later, the individual responsible for the search admitted that our data would have led to the site had it not been found by the local person. Details of this project were leaked to the press and received media attention. A few years later, President Carter reported on this incident by stating that a psychic had pinpointed the location of a missing Soviet bomber to within three miles of the actual location.

During the early days of the Fort Meade unit, one of the project viewers, Joe McMoneagle, was asked to describe activity at a location in the Soviet Union. Given only an Earth coordinate, he didn't know that it corresponded to a large assembly building. His perceptions of the area were generally correct. Then he was shown a photo of the building and asked to describe activity inside. He perceived impressions of assembly activity for a huge submarine. When asked to estimate the date of its completion, he felt it would be launched within four months. Approximately four months later, satellite photography detected the largest submarine ever built, the *Typhoon,* in a nearby harbor, where it had recently been moved from the building for sea trials. Joe had also described approximately twenty angled, or canted, missile-launch tubes. In the same building, as later learned, another submarine was being assembled. It had an unexpected feature: twenty-four angled missile-launch tubes. This information was passed on to the National Security Council staff.

During this early phase, many applications of remote viewing were used for locating equipment and describing details of emerging technical developments. Some projects included location of clandestine communication equipment in American embassies and identifying a technique of message encoding. A variety of search-application projects were also performed. One of these entailed locating a U.S. Navy plane missing in a mountainous region of the United States. A remote viewer marked an area on the map that proved to be within five miles of the actual location.

As the emerging Stargate activity became known, we were called upon more frequently. Some of these projects were intended to locate hostages and to describe their situation. These targets included the Iran hostages in 1979; Brigadier General Dozier, who was abducted by the Italian Red Brigades in 1981; and Lieutenant Colonel Higgins, who was abducted in Lebanon in 1987.

Some of the remote viewing data obtained during the Iran-hostage crisis could be verified. In one instance, Keith Harary, a remote viewer, perceived that Mr. Queen, a hostage, would be released for medical reasons within two or three days. His data included specific medical conditions. This data was passed on to the National Security Council. Two days later, Mr. Queen was unexpectedly released for the medical reasons perceived by the remote viewer.

Several remote viewers provided data that narrowed down the search possibilities for BG Dozier to the correct city and type of building. He was eventually rescued based on data provided by an informer. Remote viewing data concerning the location of L/C Higgins could be verified early on. However, it was not possible to take any action or to verify later information.

I was in Italy as part of the search team for BG Dozier. Although I performed a variety of tasks, I also integrated data from project viewers and from others providing impressions, to see if remote viewing could help identify or narrow down BG Dozier's location. Early in the search, remote viewing data was diverse and difficult to evaluate. Some remote viewers perceived that he was in "a blue tent," suggesting an outdoor location. Others perceived that he was in a large urban area. After a few weeks, the data from project viewers became consistent and specific. Several remote viewers felt that he was being held in Padua, a city in northern Italy, and provided general area sketches. Some information was very specific, such as above a store or near a university. When he was eventually rescued, we learned that he had been kept inside a tent on the second floor of an apartment directly above a large supermarket. A university was a few blocks away. I learned later that BG Dozier had deduced his location about halfway through the six weeks he was held captive. Once he knew his location in Padua, he concentrated on hopes that someone would sense, via ESP, where he was being held.

We also worked on a variety of prediction projects. In a few instances, we identified emerging terrorist acts and unexpected incidents during the Persian Gulf activity and Desert Storm. One of these included the prediction of a missile attack against the USS Stark, a destroyer in the Persian Gulf. A few days later the event actually occurred. Twenty-seven crewmen were killed and the Stark almost sank. Later, a project viewer accurately predicted an unexpected strike along the Kuwait border. Another project provided specific information about a ship in the Mediterranean that was suspected of transporting chemicals for warfare.

In one technical tip-off project, remote viewers accurately perceived at a Soviet facility construction features (large igloolike domes, mirrorlike objects) that were not yet apparent from photography. They also had impressions that the purpose of these domes was "transmitting blue light." Six months later, several large dome structures appeared. The facility was suspected to be involved in laser-system development, possibly for tracking or weapon applications.

As the Cold War wound down, we shifted focus to drug-enforcement projects. Early on we were able to locate accurately large drug shipments both at sea and while ships were in port. One of these was a large ship in the northern Pacific Ocean that carried almost ten thousand tons of marijuana. In another instance, a remote viewer located a ship in the Atlantic that was subsequently observed by a reconnaissance flight. One project led to information on how drugs were passed through a tunnel across the Mexican border into the U.S. Other projects provided data on where drugs were stored on a small island in the Caribbean and cached on a ship in port. We were asked to locate a former Drug Enforcement Agency (DEA) employee who was a fugitive wanted for drug-smuggling cooperation. One of the Stargate remote viewers narrowed down his location to northern Wyoming near a campground. Although our data was not acted upon, the fugitive was captured a few weeks later at a campground in northern Wyoming. This data was totally contrary to the DEA expectations. They believed he was hiding somewhere in the Caribbean region.

I walked around the deck that night musing about all those projects—the successes and the failures. Not everything we tried worked, especially toward the end of Stargate. Some of our data could not be put to use in time; there were times we were accurate, but not accurate enough. Still other times, only general data was sufficient, such as in narrowing down search possibilities. I knew that we had demonstrated remote viewing's potential in search projects, for providing tip-off or alert clues on emerging developments, and for insight into the status of hostages.

I recalled some of those nighttime dreams before my official connection with SRI and Stargate. They were motivating dreams that gave me confidence that psi was real and could be applied. They continued, even after I began formal remote viewing activity in 1976. One of them stands out above the others, and it gave me insight into psi's potential for detecting emerging incidents.

In the summer of 1976, I had a series of dreams that repeated the same theme: *An airplane leaves the Soviet Union in the Far East....A new Soviet airplane flies across or near South Korea, heading toward sea.* A week later, a Soviet pilot in a new MIG-25 defected, landing in Japan. There was no way I could have anticipated that event. I had not experienced similar dreams before, nor have I since, but during that time I was exploring precognitive dreams and was open to their potential.

But now Stargate was closed. I, others from the project, or new explorers could only dream of a future Stargate. Like the mythical Greek

Phoenix, I was sure Stargate, in some form or other, would rise again. Now was the time to begin an international cooperative effort. Now was the time to consider the potential of remote viewing from a global perspective through a new effort structured to be independent of political whims and strong negative biases. It was time to think about future Stargates. It was time to dream again.

I thought about our research achievements and the contribution they had made to a review of psi research by Dr. Jessica Utts, a professor of statistics at the University of California. She wrote: "Using the standards applied to any other area of science, it is concluded that psychic functioning has been well established."

In time, this conclusion will help overcome the resistance that prevails in many academic and scientific areas against remote viewing and psi phenomena. One of Stargate's greatest achievements will be its contribution to this shift in viewpoint.

Stargate research showed that targets with sharp boundaries are easier to sense via remote viewing than are uniform or bland targets. This is similar to how our senses normally function: Our eyes excel at sensing edges and motion; our ears respond to changes in air pressure.

Stargate experienced occasional cycles of support and withdrawal. At times, upper-level managers saw the project as being on the cutting edge of discovery and new applications. At others, with timid or fearful high-level managers and review officials, we had to keep a low profile and not make a wave. Management responsibilities shifted over the years, since it was unclear where we should be assigned.

The Cold War thaw brought a refocus of responsibilities within DOD. Stargate activities were reduced; external research funding was canceled. Individuals left the project to resume other careers, and in 1993 I retired to pursue writing and to present workshops on human potential topics.

A CIA-sponsored review of the program in 1995 recommended its closure. While it was reasonably objective, this review has been judged by some to have been hastily conducted and politically driven. It only examined the last two years when the program was in decline. That report led to the

"Nightline" program that flashed across my screen that November evening.

Some people have difficulty considering phenomena like remote viewing or other types of psychic experiences from a balanced viewpoint. Many strong critics assume these phenomena cannot be possible and they strive to discount all aspects of psi. Conversely, some others are too quick to accept anything that might look like a psychic event, when it may simply result from a chance occurrence or an erroneous observation. As in any venture, it is best to take small steps and to examine results in an open, unbiased way. Care and caution will not extinguish the phenomena, but they will inspire confidence for taking further steps and finding ways to apply psi in one's own life.

Over the years, many individuals helped support the Stargate project. I hope someday that credit can be given to those who desire to be recognized. (I know some will prefer to remain hidden behind the scenes. Standing tall for a topic like remote viewing is not necessarily career enhancing.) Some people, however, are aggressively open about their links to Stargate, which is creating negative impressions. By focusing on how our psi potential can help ourselves and others, the positive gains from Stargate can be brought into public awareness.

Stargate research substantiated remote viewing phenomena and its applications demonstrated that remote viewing has potential for helping in practical situations. With a balanced approach, anyone can explore the range of their own psi or remote viewing potential and discover for themselves what is or is not true.

As I progressed with Stargate research and applications, I also explored and came to know an inner Stargate. Project Stargate opened a new window—into myself, into regions that link and interconnect with others. That window is there for all of us.

Late that November night, I relived those exciting times when we made new discoveries and found what others had not. Now that Stargate was in the open, I felt a strong sense of freedom. It is now a benchmark, a reference point, making it easier for others to follow and begin their own Stargate odyssey.

I thought of my own experiences and how they let me see the reality of our psychic nature. What were the tracks I had sensed and then followed? I knew I had to write about them. For me, they were tracks in the psychic wilderness. I knew others could find them, too.

Exploring Remote Viewing

Like gravity and other natural phenomena, the phenomenon we
have been rediscovering and exploring in the laboratory has
been around since the dawn of humankind's recorded search.
...Perhaps our place in the universe is now secure enough
that we can begin to take another look at a piece of ourselves that we have long attempted to ignore.

➤ Dr. Harold Puthoff and Russell Targ, *Mind Reach* (page 212) n the early 1970s, researchers at the Stanford Research Institute (SRI), were studying claims by individuals who said they could describe distant scenes that were unknown to them when those sites were being visited by friends or colleagues. Their perceptions were found to correlate well with the place being visited. The people who were able to describe distant scenes became known as "remote viewers." Those who were visiting the scene—the "target site"—were called "beacon persons." Initially researchers suspected the person at the site served as some type of beacon to guide a remote viewer's attention toward the target. The term *remote viewing* followed from the visual type of data generally produced by the viewers, although they experienced other sensory impressions as well.

While sketches made by remote viewers had corresponded well with configurations at the target site, their attempts to analyze or name their perceptions were not as accurate. Thus, any judging of results, or potential use of remote viewing data, had to be based primarily on how well the sketch matched what was at the the actual scene, not on what the viewer thought the scene or objects were. For example, a viewer might perceive and sketch a "large white dome" and call it an observatory, when it was in fact the Capitol Building in Washington, D.C.

Around the same time, researchers discovered that a beacon person did not need to be at the target site. Precognitive remote viewing experiments were also successful. The viewer could accurately describe the site that would be selected and visited in the future. For example, at 11:00 AM, a remote viewer is asked to describe where a beacon person will be later that afternoon, at 2:00 PM. The beacon person, who does not yet know the location, will only find out where he or she is to go shortly before 2:00, when he or she randomly selects the destination from a list of many possibilities.

The beacon person then travels to that destination, making sure to arrive at 2:00, and remains at this area at least fifteen minutes, making sketches and photographs. The individual then returns to the remote viewer and compares the remote viewer's sketches, made hours earlier, with features of the actual site. In this example, there is no way anyone could know the beacon person's future destination. When successful, as many such experiments are, evidence for a mental ability for future seeing, or precognition, is demonstrated.

Other remote viewing experiments showed that only an arbitrary reference, such as an Earth coordinate, could be used for designating the target site. No one needed to visit the scene. Given only Earth coordinates, remote viewers could accurately provide details of a distant place that would not have been available from any map.

Later, other abstract designators, such as arbitrary names or numbers, were also found to enable the viewer to describe the intended target. This targeting approach made it possible to designate target areas anywhere on Earth and to have remote viewers provide relevant data about those locations. Results of this research eventually led to the Stargate program. Initial remote viewing projects were for geographic areas. Later, moving targets became of interest as well: Where is the ship, the hostage, the fugitive?

Psi phenomena have been reported for centuries. Literature has many examples of people with abilities similar to remote viewing, such as clairvoyance. In early times, experiences of this nature were thought to have their bases in the supernatural, as were most natural phenomena.

When psi phenomena were first studied systematically in the late 1800s, in England, researchers linked them with types of signal transference that were similar to a telegraph or to electromagnetic waves. It was suspected that our minds transmitted and received signals through an unknown process they named "telepathy."

Around the turn of the century, several researchers in England examined the ability of people with psi talent to describe distant scenes. Some of these experiments yielded results that were similar to those later achieved by the SRI remote viewers. All of this early work assumed that a focal person, a "sender," had to be at the distant scene. Invention of the radio and public familiarity with radio waves, strengthened the belief that psi resulted from signals being sent between brains.

In the early 1930s, psi research by Dr. J. B. Rhine at Duke University combined informational aspects of psi (such as clairvoyance and telepathy) under one label—extrasensory perception, or ESP. Most of Rhine's ESP research was based on statistical analysis with cards that had only five different symbols. His participants did not see any image of the cards; they reacted to something like a gut feeling, a hunch, or intuition, to make their selection. Results of these experiments provided statistical evidence for ESP's existence.

In the 1960s, a new approach for exploring psi was initiated at the Maimonides Medical Center in Brooklyn, New York. This research, led by Montague Ullman, Stanley Krippner, and Charles Honorton, looked for evidence of psi in the dream state. In the early 1970s, they also began to examine the relaxed state to see if people could experience psi when awake.

During these experiments, an assistant was isolated from others in the experiments and given a randomly selected target, usually an art print. For the dream experiments, he or she then observed that picture, hoping that the sleeping person would dream about the target. For the later relaxed-state experiments, that person observed the target and hoped that the relaxed person's mental imagery or other impressions would correspond to the picture. Results from over twenty years of research were statistically significant and provided evidence that psi can occur in the dream state and when relaxed.

In the relaxed-state experiments, the individuals attempting to perceive the target were encouraged to report any impressions that came to them. Since the target could be anything, the subconscious was freed from the possible interference of guessing,

Some of the Maimonides experiments showed that mental imagery during dreams or when relaxed could be highly accurate, almost like a snapshot. This suggested that a free-response approach for eliciting psi had practical application potential.

The Stanford Research Institute (SRI) remote viewing research, which was also based on a free-response approach, soon followed. In the late 1970s, psi research including remote viewing was initiated by Dean Robert Jahn at Princeton University. Remote viewing research has also been performed at the Rhine Research Center, Durham, North Carolina.

Over the years, remote viewing research has shown that:

➤ Remote viewing is not limited by distance or time;

➤ Remote viewing is a natural phenomenon that can be experienced in varying degrees by anyone;

➤ Sketches and drawings are more reliable than the interpretation of the sketches;

➤ Motivation and the perceived importance of the task are more important than any training approach; and

➤ Remote viewing data contains a mix of valid information and error ("noise"). Noise can be reduced through practice and experience.

Psi phenomena are difficult to reconcile with conventional views of physical reality. New understanding has emerged from studies in quantum physics that offers clues and helps bridge the gap between science and psi. Quantum physics points toward a holographic, wavelike nature of the universe. A hologram results from wave-interference patterns; any portion of the hologram contains the same information as does the larger hologram in toto. Distant interactions that have no conventional explanation are predicted and observed between certain coupled particles. Such effects are referred to as "nonlocal" interactions.

Quantum physics allows for an observer effect when measuring properties of elementary particles. For example, the nature of an electron can be revealed as a particle or a wave, depending on how it is observed or measured. Light also has a dual particle-or-wave nature, but not simultaneously. Certain brain activities are wavelike in nature and suggest a holographic essence.

A hologram is a thin film with recorded interference patterns from intersecting electromagnetic waves, such as light. The more the waves or frequencies are in-phase and coherent, the more distinct the resulting pattern will be.

Usually a hologram is created with laser light by bouncing a portion of its light off an object, recombining that reflected light with the original reference beam, then causing it to strike the film emulsion. After the film is developed, all that can be seen is a complex pattern of light and dark areas, much like many overlapping fingerprints. When the original laser light is passed through the hologram, the objects that were originally illuminated seem to pop out in front of the film, looking much like the real objects. When a small piece of the hologram is cut out of the larger hologram and illuminated, it also reproduces the original object or scene, although not as clearly.

The brain has functions that resemble the way a hologram works. Memory is distributed throughout large regions of the brain and is not isolated in small locations as was once believed. The process of identifying someone and memory recall both resemble a pattern-recognition process that is similar to the manner in which information is retrieved from a hologram. Skill learning has a pattern-recognition character. All our senses operate more like frequency detectors and produce wavelike electrical-interference patterns in the brain that are similar to how holograms are created.

Advances in efforts toward the unification of the laws of physics may offer insight into all natural phenomena, including time. Concepts have been proposed such as hidden variables that contain universal patterns or unifying principles. Holomovements, implicate order, and morphogenic fields are some terms used to describe them. These concepts hint at information exchange being a basic interaction among matter, biological systems, and possibly consciousness.

A new concept—string theory—considers the universe to be a sea of microscopic "strings" that vibrate, thus forming elementary particles. This is another approach for considering the wavelike nature of the universe to be its fundamental property. Wavelike resonances may be the link between matter and consciousness—and psi phenomena.

These observations and concepts, along with anticipated discoveries, may eventually lead us to understand the nature of the universe better and comprehend how consciousness interacts with matter or energy. These advances may help in our arriving at an understanding of the nature of psi phenomena.

Remote viewing and other psi phenomena remind us that our comprehension of the universe is incomplete. Psi, in general, may have a holographic or wavelike nature that is similar to light. "Psi waves" might be the means for accessing a mindlike hologram that, like gravity, extends throughout the universe.

The term *remote viewing* is gaining wider acceptance. Many psi practitioners routinely follow a remote viewing approach in their activities. Some professionals are adding remote viewing as an extra tool to help them in their daily work. Books are now published that describe how remote viewing has helped in some archaeological explorations and in police detective projects. A few individuals in counselling work have reported on how remote viewing impressions have give them insight for their casework. Researchers continue to examine remote viewing. Accounts of spontaneous remote viewing occurrences are being reported by the media and in specialized literature. In the years ahead, we can anticipate that more people will discover their inherent remote viewing talent.

1
Ohio Caverns

A NEW OR UNUSUAL EXPERIENCE USUALLY REMAINS VIVID IN MEMORY THROUGHOUT our lives. I'm sure we can all recall the essence, even details, of that first day in school, first date, or first presentation. Both positive and negative events, when charged with strong emotion or special significance, are never far from the surface of our consciousness. Certain startling experiences, especially those that run contrary to our notion of reality, have a similar effect. My first encounter with remote viewing phenomenon left just such a lasting impression with me. I occasionally review that experience, reliving its impact. Although I was only an observer, the event was a turning point in my life. It motivated me to move deeper into an inner voyage of discovery.

My professional career of aerospace engineering and physics left little room for the subjective, though I was certainly aware of creativity, intuitive flashes, and occasional unusual coincidences. At that time I believed there was some purely rational basis for these "soft experiences." The laws of chance, it seemed, could account for all coincidences. Some of my childhood experiences were puzzling and suggested a psi origin. However, I eventually accepted a conventional view of reality and disregarded them.

In 1976, when I became contract manager for remote viewing research, one of my first actions was to set up and observe a viewing experiment. The principal researchers at SRI, Dr. Harold Puthoff and Russell Targ, visited Dayton and put me in phone contact with Hella Hammid, a project remote viewer, while she was visiting in New York City. Hella lived in Los Angeles and was a professional photographer.

Calling her from Dayton, I introduced myself as a colleague of Hal's and invited her to participate in a remote viewing experiment later that day. She was eager to see what she could do. All she knew was that we could be anywhere in the U.S. We had never met and she did not know where I lived or worked.

Earlier that day I had prepared a list of ten diverse places in the Dayton area that would be good potential remote viewing targets. They included sites on Wright Patterson Air Force Base as well as locations around the city. I intended to select one of them at random shortly before Hal, Russ, and I went there as beacon persons. I made sure that Hal and Russ did not know what targets were on my list. I didn't want to risk possible criticism that they might have inadvertently given clues of my target possibilities to Hella. If Hella succeeded, a critic might claim her success was due to a good guess rather than remote viewing.

Although Hella sounded very enthusiastic, friendly, and cooperative, I felt somewhat uncomfortable. I could only hope my feelings of doubt would not affect the experiment. Much depended on this event, even though it could only serve as a demonstration of remote viewing—not as proof— should the results turn out to be successful. Likewise, a failure would not negate remote viewing. I needed to be reasonably convinced that some-thing of potential use could result from this research. Otherwise I might not get the project off to a good start. I had many pressing demands on my time and I suspected that working on a topic as way-out as remote viewing would give me plenty of headaches.

Since I was not experienced at selecting targets, I began to have doubts about how I had constructed that target pool. As I reviewed them, I realized many sites had similar features, differing only in scale or size. The Air Force Logistics Command building, though larger, resembles the Air Force Institute of Technology Headquarters, which I had on my list. The old Dayton Post Office has large steps and columns similar to those at the Xenia Courthouse, though not as many. Others were too complex and would be too busy and confusing to Hella, or they could fit most anything she described. For a simple demonstration, these technical problems may not have mattered, but I need-ed to observe something more convincing than how well a few of Hella's sketches might match assorted buildings or structures in the Dayton area. I wanted to observe an unambiguous, successful remote viewing experiment.

As I pondered this dilemma, an idea hit me: Why not select a truly unique target? And if it were some distance from Dayton, then it couldn't be argued that Hella might have known where Hal was visiting and had simply made a good guess. It was good idea, but what could be such a target?

Pacing around, a great target occurred to me. Very unique and very isolated, it was thirty-five miles away, near Columbus, Ohio. I rounded up Hal and Russ and proceeded to drive out of Dayton. They were curious about the location of my target, since they suspected I had selected a site somewhere on base. I drove on silently, keeping the destination to myself. They were quite surprised when I pulled into the parking lot of the Ohio Caverns.

"This is a great target!" exclaimed Hal, "We have never attempted a cave or anything underground. Hella ought to enjoy this."

I was pleased to hear such confidence. I still had many doubts.

Taking in the scenery on the cavern grounds, Russ pointed out another advantage to using this site as the target. It would give us an opportunity to observe how a remote viewer would do when describing someone who is underground, where low-frequency waves are highly attenuated. Some theorists, including Soviet ESP researcher I. M. Kogan, had proposed that low-frequency brain waves have a role in psi.

We daydreamed about doing a remote viewing experiment from a submarine, since seawater blocks out most electromagnetic radiation. Remote viewing success with a submarine deep in the ocean would rule out electromagnetics as a carrier of psi information. (Later in the program, fortuitous circumstances would permit us to carry out just such an experiment.)

We had coffee, then joined a tour shortly before the time Hella would begin her remote viewing six hundred miles away. Slowly we strolled through archways of overhanging vines, entered through a narrow doorway, and descended into the darkness of Ohio's largest cavern, formed eons ago by water dissolving limestone under the rolling hillsides of central Ohio. We were surrounded by tall white and beige stalagmites jutting up from the ground; similar-looking stalactites loomed down from the dark ceiling. They reflected a golden glow from hundreds of bare bulbs stretching along the passageways.

We moved slowly through the cave, chilled by the cold, misty air, inching across slippery paths, squeezing through a maze of rocky tunnels, and crossing shaky bridges that spanned crystal clear pools. Water dripped from the high ceiling. Occasionally, the tour guide called for silence and turned off the lights. In this dark, eerie vault, it was easy to feel primeval connections to the earth's chaotic origin, to the steady flow of time and evolution.

I could not help feeling a deep sense of awe, of mystery. Occasionally, my musings drifted toward Hella. I wondered if she had linked up with us, and how she might be experiencing, or interpreting, our adventure into this fascinating deep cave. There was no question: She would either be right on or way off. This experiment would either be a hit or a miss.

After forty-five minutes, we came to the cave exit. Steep metal stairs angled toward the faint light of the outside world 150 feet above. A loud, metallic booming echoed as we stomped upward. We filed through a heavy metal door and emerged into a bright, sunny afternoon, shielding and blinking our eyes. The tour guide heaved the massive door shut.

At the agreed-upon time, I placed a call to Hella. My anxiety grew to an almost intolerable level as the phone rang and rang. Finally she answered.

"We are through visiting the site, Hella. What did you see?" I asked.

Our protocol was just to listen to Hella and give no feedback until after we had received her written material. I waited anxiously for her reply.

"This is strange....I don't know what you guys got yourselves into. It sure is scary! I saw...a maze of caves...brightly lit. You were in a misty place...deep underground."

I remained quiet, motionless, hardly believing what I was hearing. How could she sense our site so well? There was no doubt; she had sensed the exact nature of the Ohio Caverns. She continued describing her impressions.

"At first I saw something like a wine cellar entrance, and an archway with wisteria, leading to an underground world. Then I saw caves, or mines ...deep shafts...an earthy smell...moist passages. Silent, not much sound ...scary...a golden glow all over. Only a few people. A very special place."

She paused briefly, as though reliving her experience, then continued: "There is something humming, throbbing.... You come to...a steel wall."

She remained quiet, no doubt anxious about how she had done. I thanked her, being careful not to show a reaction, and told her she would know the target as soon as we received her written scripts. I hung up and slowly turned to Hal and Russ, shaking my head.

"She got it! She got the target! I can't believe this. She was right on!"

Hal and Russ were elated. They knew it was important for me to see remote viewing first hand. I drove back to Dayton slowly. We talked continuously about the experiment, seeing it as a benchmark. For me, it certainly was significant. With a few brief, excitement-filled words, Hella had brought me directly into the world of remote viewing. I could sense her enthusiasm and courage. My solid view of reality had to bend a little. I now had to make room for a deeper level of awareness I had suppressed and ignored.

Hal, Russ, and I talked of the many challenges ahead, and how to best apply remote viewing. Could we find a way to improve accuracy? Could remote viewers do better in identifying or interpreting their perceptions? We had a lot to think about.

Back in Dayton, I turned to Hal and said: "Why don't we credit this experiment to Hella by naming it 'Hella's Cave'?"

"I think she'll be pleased," he said.

"And she didn't have to pay for the tour," I quipped.

We received Hella's written scripts several days later. After her remote viewing session, she had attempted to interpret her impressions. She thought our "scary place" was something "far out," possibly an entrance to an "underground city" or something "nuclear." It is not uncommon for remote viewers to miss the analytical aspects of the target. Specific names, numbers, and functions are difficult for remote viewers to detect and are not nearly as reliable as drawings or sketches. Even though she missed the function of our recreational site, she had most everything else correct.

While positive proof could not be derived from just one experiment, Hella's Cave gave me an unforgettable reference point. I now found the confidence I needed to continue with my emerging remote viewing activity. Feeling a new dedication, I knew I could give this effort whatever professional energy it demanded. Now I was willing to square off with the critics.

I had taken Hal and Russ into that cave to explore the boundaries of remote viewing, but that misty cave also brought me closer to unknown dimensions deep within myself. Hella's Cave was my initiation into remote viewing and helped begin an exciting adventure—a voyage of inner discovery.

2

The Challenge

SHORTLY AFTER I MET HAL PUTHOFF IN 1976, HE INVITED ME TO VISIT HIM AT SRI TO meet his staff and to learn details on his research. This was to be my first visit to a parapsychology laboratory and I looked forward to the opportunity with great enthusiasm. My only previous awareness of psi research was through books written by Dr. John B. Rhine and a more recent one written on the dream telepathy investigations at the Maimonides Medical Center in Brooklyn, New York. When I read these books, I was quite surprised to learn that anyone was taking psi phenomena seriously.

Even though the psi researchers represented only a handful of people, they struck me as being highly dedicated, innovative, and courageous. Their activity was openly opposed by the conventional scientific community and certain religious groups also attacked their efforts. It seemed that, if proven to be true, psi phenomena would have a tremendous impact not only on our understanding of the physical universe, but on our own psychic potential as well. I considered psi research to be a frontier science—an attempt to bridge age-old mysteries of the human psyche with fundamental principles of the universe. Psi researchers were explorers, examining the boundaries of both the mental and the physical.

That first visit to SRI was a milestone event for me. I had long discussions with all the staff, asked many questions, reviewed their research, and observed several remote viewing experiments. I plunged into historical journals of psi investigations, which started in 1882 when the Society for Psychical Research was founded in London.

Then came the challenge. I had not been aware of Hal's policy of having visitors try their own, often hidden, remote viewing talents to learn the protocol directly and to see for themselves that psi is a widespread natural talent that is not restricted to a few superstars. Toward the end of my visit, he told me it was time for me to do remote viewing, not only read about it.

"C'mon, Hal," I protested. "I can't do remote viewing. Others can, but that's not my bag. Let me stick with studying your work and pondering it's significance."

"Sorry," he said, firmly. "Experience has shown that those who visit us to review our program can also do well. Direct participation reduces, even eliminates, their suspicions that we may be doing something wrong. When people who have never done remote viewing before do well with our protocol, they know first-hand what remote viewing is like. Then they can't try to explain away our results, or stand in awe of some superstar. Experience is always the best teacher.

"Haven't you seen by now that remote viewing is a natural talent? So why can't anyone, including you, do it? I thought you were an adventurous individual."

His last remark got me. Of course I was adventuresome! Of course I was willing to take risks, to explore. That was my basic nature, so why not explore my own remote viewing potential?

I scowled at him and said: "Okay, Hal, I'll play this silly game. I'll show you what a fool I am."

"Good! Now I know you will do well. Let's go at it this afternoon."

I took a long lunch break and paced around the SRI grounds. What had I agreed to do? Why should I try something as way out as remote viewing? I always had great difficulty relaxing. How could I even get into a calm, receptive state in thirty short minutes? If nothing happened, I rationalized, at least it would be a pleasant rest and I would have demonstrated to Hal that not everyone can do remote viewing.

Still, I resisted. Why? I had seen others do well. How could I forget Hella's Cave? I was certainly interested in psi research. I understood the potential of remote viewing...for anyone. Why exclude myself?

Since I resisted personally experiencing remote viewing, I was sure I was not on some type of ego trip, as I suspected of some psi practitioners I read about.

If I was not interested in psi for some hidden agenda, then why was I so anxious? Why did I resist the notion of doing remote viewing? I felt I was leading a balanced lifestyle, and would not overact to uncovering any remote viewing ability I might have.

Strolling along, it struck me that perhaps I harbored some hidden fear. I was sure my anxiety was not due to suspected inability to control remote viewing phenomena. A parapsychologist, Dr. Charles Tart, had found evidence through interviews that some people resist psi because they fear losing control over it. A few people I had talked to in the community when I was sampling opinions about the "Psychic Realm" course that I was considering teaching expressed a similar concern. However, I had painstakingly examined decades worth of research, had talked to accomplished sensitives and read their autobiographies, and I had discovered nothing that supported this concern. Research demonstrated that psi is generally a suppressed phenomenon. People who describe troubling psi experiences probably let their own fantasies get in the way. I did not see loss of control over psi—by myself or others—as anything that warranted such concern.

Maybe I was afraid of other people's opinions of remote viewing. It certainly was no secret that some leading scientists and religious spokespeople positioned themselves solidly against psi or anything that resembled it. After studying their arguments, it became clear to me that their motivation was not to explore openly, to see what is there, which is the truly scientific and common sense approach, but rather to shut off the search for truth.

In a sense, such scientists were simply espousing scientism—science as fixed, science as religion. Some of the religious people who are critical of psi, it seemed to me, were most concerned about preserving certain ancient interpretations of reality, some of which were clearly fear-based. Or perhaps they were driven by the need to control, a tendency that eventually happens in any organization, especially when similar but competing groups emerge as perceived threats. It was also possible that some of these people were fearful because they viewed psi phenomena as being in the realm of the supernatural.

I thought I had worked all that out for myself and that I understood why some people resist psi. Was I avoiding the real issue? Simply put, did I fear failure? Was I afraid of looking bad, of looking like a fool?

The more I considered my concern about "looking foolish," the more humorous my situation appeared. Of course I could, would, *will* look foolish! Didn't I look terrible during my first few tennis games, when I slammed the ball high over the fence or straight down on my toes? But still, I had broken out laughing at my clumsy actions, which then helped me to calm down, to get past the fears of not doing well so that I could let the game flow.

I had to forget, or at least suspend and ignore that terrifying inner judge who didn't like it when I looked foolish. Push my self-consciousness off to the side, where, though not totally removed, it would be sufficiently detached to permit those mysterious inner processes we call up when learning anything to have a chance to do their thing. After I had tripped over my feet a few times, I went on in the weeks that followed to accurately drive tennis balls all over the court.

What I needed to do now was lighten up, relax, laugh. It didn't matter if I did well or not this first time, or the second, or the one-hundredth. As long as I kept trying, I was sure something would happen. Psi would surface; I could examine its tracks, learn more about the process, and apply it in my own life. After all, the vision of applying psi to help others was what had peaked my interest in this phenomenon initially. There were new boundaries to be explored and I had to jump in myself in order to find out what they were.

As I returned to the SRI lab, I felt a new enthusiasm. I had a winning companion with me—humor. All I had to do was laugh and let those tensions fly away. I couldn't help chuckling as I walked into the building.

Hal sensed my odd demeanor. "Okay, where did you go for lunch? Some funny farm?"

"No, Hal. That may come later, " I kidded. "Remember what I said about looking foolish this morning ? I was on track. I will indeed look foolish during this remote viewing experiment. Let me go and prove it. Come on, let's get it over with!"

"Good. I can see you are ready!"

The door to the comfortable, dimly lit remote viewing room closed. I was accompanied by Russ, whose only function was to prompt me occasionally by saying "Describe the target," and to ensure that I didn't fall asleep. Russ had no knowledge of what the target would be. All I knew was that Hal would be visiting a randomly selected site somewhere in the San Francisco Bay area. The target could be anything.

I sat upright on a comfortable chair and took a few deep breaths, focusing on relaxing and reaching a calm state. At first I had trouble keeping my analytical mind out of the way. I had suspended my "super judge," but now I had to wrestle with my tendency toward analysis. I became concerned that my innate curiosity might block the remote viewing process, so I had to send my curiosity off to the sidelines, too.

After a few minutes of reasonable calm, I began to see faint traces of something. I could not help being curious about these inner perceptions and tried to interpret anything that popped into view. What were those faint light flashes? What about the odd lines and dots of light? Even though I was aware of normal visual phenomena (called "photisms"), I hadn't experienced them before. No, those were not of the target, they were issuing from me. I could see how people might misinterpret them as arising from beyond themselves. Pushing analysis aside, I slipped into a more relaxed state and patiently waited. Keeping my eyes closed, I was only dimly aware of Russ's monotone: "Describe...the...target."

After some time, my analytical mind-partner remained at the sidelines along with its super-judge counterpart. I dropped deeper into a relaxed state, and had to guard against falling asleep.

I faintly heard Russ repeat the request: "Describe...the ...target."

Suddenly, I saw vague images. Since they were not at all clear, I was concerned that my imagination was now coming on stage. Did I also have to send my imagination mind-partner to the bleachers? I told Russ that I saw "funny lines." Faintly, I heard Russ ask, "Can you sketch any of those funny lines—those images—that you see?"

As if in slow motion, I began to sketch "funny lines" on the paper in front of me. This took some attention and I slipped out of my relaxed state. After making my sketch, I refocused on relaxing and soon other faint images zipped in and out of my visual field. It was like looking into dark shadows and catching glints of faint, reflected light. After several minutes I began to feel disappointment—certainly nothing dramatic or vivid had happened.

Then I heard Russ say, "Okay, we are about to complete this remote viewing session. Look around again where Hal is standing. What else do you see?"

In sports, that last-minute shot, that "Hail Mary Pass," sometimes succeeds. Even in routine learning tasks, when we know the effort is nearing an end, we usually do better. Immediately after Russ's statement, I was surprised to see another image. It was still not too clear, but I could discern boundaries and the basic shape. I caught a glimpse of a large building that I thought I recognized from an earlier drive in Menlo Park, but I felt this may have been my imagination mind-partner nudging in. I was not deeply relaxed, and thought I might be beginning to invent. Maybe I was trying to figure out Hal's location too soon. Premature analysis was found to be the largest error source in remote viewing data, especially for novices.

"This remote viewing session is now over," I heard Russ say.

As I was not accustomed to long periods of relaxation, I felt drowsy and a bit spaced-out. In a few moments, I looked at what I had drawn and written. All I had drawn was a long thin band that I had noted as a "walkway" surrounded by a "sunken garden." I wrote about, but did not draw, what I thought was a tall building in Menlo Park. "There's not much here, Russ," I said, disappointed.

"Maybe there is, maybe there isn't," he responded. "When Hal returns, let's visit the target and take a look."

Soon I was in a car with Hal and Russ. We rode in silence. Hal pulled into a parking lot next to the Baylands Nature Preserve, a vast tidal basin. There were few distinguishing landmarks, only a wide-open stretch of swamp. A thin, long, straight boardwalk led out into the bog several feet above the wetland flora.

I had mixed feelings. My sketches were not detailed enough for me to feel that I had "connected" with the target. My sense of a "sunken garden" was very general, and may have captured some essence of the tidal basin. Hal had been pacing back and forth along the narrow boardwalk, looking around, and down into the tidal flats. Straight ahead of the boardwalk, well in the distance, loomed a tall structure—the Menlo Park Municipal Building—but that was visible from many places in the area.

Hal and Russ felt I had sensed some elements, or gestalts, of the target area. I was not convinced. The target was simple, so were my perceptions. I needed to see better results before I could accept my own latent remote viewing ability.

Like my first tennis games, maybe I had begun to reach out toward these new boundaries and had caught a glimpse of the target area. I had to take a closer look; I had to continue exploring those boundaries.

"Okay, Hal," I said, "that was a warm-up. I would like to try again. How about tomorrow morning?"

"Great," he responded. "I knew you would overcome your resistance. Let's talk about this over dinner." In principle, relaxing should be refreshing and energizing, but I felt drained. I didn't know if this was from the inner effort to keep blocks out of the way, or something inherent to the remote viewing process itself.

The next morning I woke refreshed, energetic, and eager to tackle my second attempt at remote viewing. I ate lightly, held back on coffee, and took a long, relaxing morning walk. I was beginning to understand the importance of exercise and humor for well-being and for keeping balance. A balanced lifestyle also helps attain calm states. Relaxing was the key for opening the remote viewing flow along with sending fears, inner judges, and quick analyses to the sidelines.

Our procedure for my second remote viewing experiment was the same, but this time it was much easier for me to get into the experiment, to relax. Maybe my first session had served mainly to work out a few jitters, something like stage fright.

Soon the door closed and Russ spoke to me and the tape recorder in his monotone. "You are now ready to begin today's remote viewing session. Describe the target." I had little difficulty relaxing and holding onto the goal: Where was Hal? What was he looking at? What were the key features of the target area? Occasionally I thought of a constraint: I didn't want impressions unrelated to the target. I aimed to be as accurate as possible and was sure my subconscious could accommodate that.

In my inner vision, I saw many complex forms and shapes. Some of the configurations were vivid, others were faint. Maybe the target had a wide range of resolution demands. At times, I suspected my imagination was trying to fill in the blanks, and I sent it off to the sidelines. I was only vaguely aware of Russ's frequent requests to describe the target.

At first, the images were fragmentary; then they formed discernible patterns and shapes. I attempted to make a composite and put them into proper spatial relationships. I could only write descriptive words for some impressions, since I could not draw them accurately. This time, I did not feel that my sketching interfered with my inner perceptions. I found a balance: sketch, then wait with high expectation, then sketch. I was not in a very deep state of relaxation.

Almost before I realized what had happened, the session was over. I heard Russ's voice: "Okay, time to wrap it up. Finish your sketches, then when Hal returns, we will go see how well you did this time." I liked Russ's positive attitude.

I had drawn what looked like a very complex courtyard scene—many buildings surrounding a large central area. One large building dominated numerous smaller ones. I also saw several archways and neatly configured stone walls. I glimpsed many bicycles and lots of tall plants in the open, central area. The tall building was confusing; I sensed plants toward the top, not at the base, which gave the impression of a hanging garden.

If my impressions were on track, then Hal was not at a simple target. As I looked at my drawing, I suspected the site was a shopping mall or a courtyard at some large apartment complex. I tried not to analyze during the session, but now it was alright to try to figure out where he had been.

Hal walked in. "Okay. Let's go see how well you did." It was clear that even if my results were way off, that would not bother Hal or Russ. We would simply try again, with the same high degree of optimism.

When we pulled into the campus of Stanford University, I was not surprised. Of course, Hal had been walking around in a large campus court-yard! I tried not to show too much emotion as Hal led me into the inner quadrangle. In front of me was the scene I had attempted to draw! My sketches could only approximate the images I had perceived, but I still had them in memory and could see many direct correlations. The bicycles I had glimpsed should have been a clue that Hal was at a campus and not a mall or apartment complex.

When I looked at the only tall building in the vicinity, it was easy to see it was a large church. I had not sensed that. However, on the upper-story, outside wall were large murals depicting religious figures standing under trees and tall plants. From a distance, the paintings resembled hanging gardens.

"You did great!" exclaimed Hal. "I walked around here in the center of the courtyard, hoping you would see me here. Your sketches are right on; you even have the right spatial relationships. We'll name this place 'D. G.'s Inner Quadrangle.'"

Even though my sketches for both remote viewings were basic, I could see their potential utility. They could have helped narrow down search possibilities had someone been lost in a tidal area, or held captive in or near a large plaza.

These two experiments, along with many others I observed, demon-strated that anyone could do remote viewing if they chose. I also realized that the case for, or against, remote viewing utility does not rest merely on a few demonstrations.

While my initial purpose had not been to explore remote viewing in order to develop my own talents, I was happy to learn that I could do remote viewing once in a while. Maybe my own use of remote viewing or other forms of psi would help me in personal endeavors, but at this time I wanted to see what those more experienced in remote viewing could do. I wanted to help them, to see if they could contribute to understanding psi phenomena, and if they could help advance psi's application potential.

3

Surprise at the Library

"HELLO, MY NAME IS DIANE. I HEAR THAT YOU'RE INTERESTED IN PSYCHIC PHENOMENA …and that you conduct ESP experiments."

I glanced up from my desk. She was neatly dressed in a blue Air Force uniform. Startled by her question, I asked cautiously: "Where did you hear that?"

Diane's visit occurred a few months after I became the government's project manager for the SRI remote viewing research. Only a few people were supposed to be aware of this effort.

Her response was reassuring: "I saw the announcement for the 'Psychic Realm' course you will be teaching in Beavercreek. I would like to attend, but have a conflict the evening of your class."

I had decided to teach this course in an evening education program to see if anyone in the community had an interest in psi topics and to learn of their experiences. The psi field was still new to me and I anticipated that teaching it would be a great way to learn. I intended to give all participants the option of doing psi experiments and wondered if any local people had repeatable psi talent. If they did, I anticipated replicating SRI's remote viewing experiments as a check on their claims. Critics were quite vocal in attacking the research at SRI as not being repeatable by anyone else. I also had some concern that my course would lead to speculation about Air Force interest in psi, but decided to take that risk.

Diane did not respond immediately. Gradually it occurred to me that her seeking me out could indicate more than a casual interest in the topic. Maybe she had psi experiences and needed to talk about them. I had already learned that talking about psi was not something you do with just anyone. If she had psi talents, then maybe I could begin exploring SRI's claims immediately. Perhaps Diane could help by doing remote viewing . . . right now. I knew she had security clearances since she was a member of the Air Force in my organization. If she did well in my remote viewing experiments, I anticipated involving her in official remote viewing research and applications projects.

"I guess you're in the right place, Diane. I'm glad you dropped by," I said, trying to restrain my enthusiasm.

She told me why she was interested in psychic phenomena. During her childhood, she had many premonitions that came true and she had always considered herself to be sensitive and intuitive. Several of these experiences were very dramatic, including what appeared to be incidents of psychokinesis, or mind–matter interactions. Diane told me about a recent incident where a picture had fallen from the wall when she was angry at the person shown in the picture.

We had a long discussion late into the day in my office. She eagerly agreed to explore remote viewing. I gave her research reports and other references, such as the classic *Mental Radio* (1929) by Upton Sinclair, an account of experiments, similar to remote viewing, that his wife, Mary Craig, had undertaken successfully. I was sure Mary Craig's experiences would help motivate Diane for our forthcoming remote viewing investigations. A few days later I set up a series of remote viewing projects for lunch periods and early evenings.

For the first experiment, I chose a site in downtown Dayton. Diane had no knowledge of my target pool—the sites could be anywhere within a twenty-mile radius of our office area. She was to relax in a distraction-free room in her home, intend to have impressions about my environment at the agreed-upon time, and sketch whatever images came to her. Hopefully she would sense key elements of the target. I cautioned her not to try to analyze or name things too quickly, and encouraged her to simply sketch whatever images she perceived.

Early in the SRI remote viewing research, almost total emphasis had been placed on the visual aspects of our viewers' perception. Sketches of forms and shapes were the primary output sought from them. However, the Hella's Cave experiment alerted me to the possibility that more than shapes or configurations were sensed through remote viewing. Hella had actually felt important elements of the cavern's ambience. I even thought of changing the term *remote viewing* to *remote* (or *extended*) *perception* in order to include other sensory aspects, such as sounds or feelings, that might be experienced during a remote viewing session.

I left the office the evening of my experiment with Diane and headed toward the Dayton Library, my target site, a good beginning remote viewing target. This multistory, modern building had no close counterparts in the Dayton–Xenia area. It had several clear architectural features and was located on a large city block surrounded by open areas. Thick bushes and small trees surrounded the building. Other possibilities in my target pool included the Miami River; the Old Dayton Post Office, which was fronted by many classical columns; the city tennis courts; an old church with an onion-shaped dome; and several other sites with distinct aspects. If Diane had remote viewing talent, someone looking at only her sketch should be able to select the Dayton Library from my pool as the likely target.

I arrived at the library fifteen minutes ahead of schedule to accommodate for possible traffic delays. The extra time allowed me, the beacon person, to get into the mood of the experiment. Wanting Diane to succeed, I put intense feelings into those thoughts. With my eyes closed, I visualized the library and envisioned Diane drawing an accurate sketch.

At this stage in my remote viewing research, I was not sure what role, if any, a beacon person plays in the remote viewing process. Did the remote viewer "do it all," or were others somehow helping the remote viewer access the target? Does the remote viewer sense target elements from the mind of the beacon person or from shapes or forms at the target scene? Could telepathy—a psi ability for sensing distant feelings or thoughts directly from someone else's mind—be the mechanism?

Although some researchers believed that remote viewing did not have a telepathic aspect, I was not so sure. Any psi application had to distinguish between someone's intent or belief, which may not be accurate, and the "real truth." I saw this as a critical point that had to be clarified before any serious attempts could be made to apply remote viewing, or any other from of psi. Otherwise, the reliability of the experiments could be called into question: Is the psi "sensitive" accessing supposition—correct or incorrect—already held by the police chief? Is the remote viewer perceiving knowledge in the data analyst's mind, or is the information from some independent source? This issue would drive my own investigations. It became central to the open research that I eventually helped initiate: What is the role, if any, of the sender, or beacon person, which became known as the "sender–no sender" issue.

I had other questions: How does psi work? Is precognition the fundamental phenomenon, with remote viewing (or clairvoyance or telepathy) simply one aspect? How does the remote viewer find the target? Does the beacon person or someone else in the environment help the remote viewer locate the target? Do we have a deep, subconscious, holographic mechanism that links all people and places together?

I mused over these fundamental concerns as I paced near the Dayton Library. The only approach clear to me was simply to do remote viewing. Develop an extensive database. Examine viewpoints of accomplished sensitives. Consider viewpoints from a variety of sources, new or ancient. Put the theories, claims, and speculations to the test.

I drifted into a daydreamlike state and lost track of time. When I checked my watch, I was surprised to find twenty minutes had passed. I refocused on the experiment, again wishing Diane success. I slowly walked near a corner of the building, trying not to draw attention. Hal Puthoff had told me stories of people calling the police to have them check up on a "suspicious person"—the beacon person— wandering around, "casing their place."

Shortly before the agreed upon sign-off time, I decided to press my hand on the sharp corner of the building. Perhaps that physical act could be sensed by Diane and help her identify physical aspects of the target. I stepped toward the building, pushing aside thick branches from bushes clustered against the walls. Without warning, a man leapt up from under the bushes, glaring at me! His clothes were dark and dirty; his face unshaven. He pushed the branches aside and stepped toward me, waving his fist, cursing loudly. His intentions seemed clear. I dashed around the corner and ran up the wide steps into the library. He did not follow.

In a few moments, my initial fright subsided. I had probably disturbed a sleeping homeless man who thought I was a police officer intending to round him up. He probably meant me no harm. After a few moments, I left the library. There was no sign of the man.

While driving home, I began to wonder if Diane's sketch, if she had any, would look like the Dayton Library. Had any aspects of my brief panic from the unexpected incident been transmitted? If so, what was their source—from the library's environment? From mental or emotional signals I had sent out? From that angry man? From something else? I pondered these issues late into the night. Diane and I had planned to meet in my office at noon the next day to review her first remote viewing experiment. I could hardly wait.

I glanced at Diane as she walked into my office, trying to sense how she felt. She glanced at the wall, the desk, and then toward me. I was sure she was anxious, perhaps out of concern about not doing well on her first remote viewing exercise. She sat down slowly, tightly holding a file folder.

For a while we chatted about routine matters and her work assignment. I noticed her tension lessen. When she seemed comfortable and at ease, I asked: "Well, Diane, were you able to relax at home and work on our experiment last evening?"

She sat motionless, hesitating. "Yes, but I'm not sure..."

"Diane," I interrupted, "don't be concerned about not succeeding on your first attempt at remote viewing." I wanted to assure her that it was okay to fail, as well as to succeed. I explained that we were simply exploring, and that her remote viewing attempt was intended to help her become familiar with inner perceptions. Reminding her that, as with any skill, you learn by doing and improve with practice, I explained about the many parameters that could affect remote viewing performance. For example, she may have had difficulty relaxing or did not like the target.

"I understand all that," she said softly. "I had no trouble relaxing, but I only saw a few images. I expected to be looking at something complex, maybe here on the Air Force base."

"Don't let your expectations do you in, Diane." I took a few minutes to re-emphasize a few points we had discussed. The target could be anything, large or small, simple or complex. It did not matter. That is the strength of this free-response remote viewing approach. When you allow your subconscious to roam freely, to be receptive to whatever is there, remote viewing can begin. But with preconceived notions or expectations, the remote viewing process may be blocked or distorted.

"Okay," she said, "I know my initial expectations did not influence my impressions. What I sensed is not on the base. Here are my sketches. This is everything that came to me, but . . ."

"Please, Diane, no 'buts,'" I said firmly. "If they are wrong, that's okay."

She clearly lacked confidence, as most people do when they begin remote viewing or any other new task. I reached for the folder, sensing a slight hesitance from her. Maybe she was still uncomfortable with the concept of remote viewing, or possibly with me.

Opening the folder, I casually glanced at the contents—a single sheet of plain white paper with a few sketches. A slight shockwave raced through me. She had drawn the basic configuration of the Dayton Library building! Her sketch clearly showed the shape of the building, including the multistoried reach, and the tall, thin windows. At the base of the building, she had sketched and written, "bushes and trees." I was sure that anyone familiar with Dayton would have recognized her sketch as being like the new Dayton Library building.

"Diane, this is great! Your sketch is right on. It resembles the building I was looking at. Congratulations!"

Shared enthusiasm is vital to any creative activity. Sports certainly has examples of that. This was no time to be detached. Tighter protocol and analysis could come later, but first we had to "catch good psi."

"Let's discuss your first remote viewing success over coffee. I'll treat." It was important that she absorb the feelings of success as long as possible. I was sure that this reinforcement would help her in future projects.

We picked up our coffee at the snack bar counter and found a table. Placing her sketch on the table, I asked, "Do you think you can identify the target?"

"No," she replied hesitatingly, "It may be in downtown Dayton. I'm new here and don't know the area that well. I can say this for sure, it is not in Fairborn, Xenia, or Beavercreek. It's a tall building. I don't think you were at a park or one of the rivers or lakes around here."

I told her where I had been and showed her a picture of the library. As she studied the picture, a smile crept over her face. "Yes! That's what I saw! I didn't draw it well enough. Sorry."

Taking a sip of coffee, I glanced at her. "Don't be sorry! That was a great first attempt.

"Do you see the potential here, Diane? Suppose a child had been kidnapped and held hostage in or near a large modern building that looked like your sketch? Wouldn't a sketch like this help narrow down search possibilities—especially if the police or FBI had no leads to go on? Suppose I had been held hostage while I was at the library yesterday evening. Your sketch would have eliminated a huge chunk of possibilities. Someone who knew the area could possibly have found me. Anyone with repeatable psi talent, which I suspect you have, can help solve pressing crime problems or help locate children who have wandered away."

She nodded, agreeing with my vision.

"You know, Diane, sometimes airplanes become lost. Remote viewing could help find missing pilots."

"What about prisoners of war or hostages held by terrorists?" she quickly interjected.

I could see we had a lot to talk about.

Before we left the snack bar, I took another look at her sketch.

"Don't forget to drop by the library as soon as you can," I reminded her. "Walking around the real place is better than looking at this photo. That direct feedback will give you more confidence and will strengthen the remote viewing process for you."

"Paul and I will be going downtown this weekend. I'll certainly visit the library. They may even have a few good books!" she quipped.

"They do," I replied , "but not too many on psi phenomena or research, I'm afraid. Maybe in time that will change."

"By the way, I do have one more question about your drawings," I said cautiously. "I don't quite understand these squiggles where you drew the bushes. Were you trying to write something?"

She seemed perplexed. I wondered if she still had some anxieties about doing remote viewing?

"I almost left out those squiggles," she said. "You see, something happened that I was sure had nothing to do with the experiment. Maybe I do have some hidden fears...."

Her voice trailed off. This puzzled me. After my enthusiastic response to her results, and her equally enthusiastic reaction, what could be wrong?

"Maybe I do have some concerns about remote viewing," she said, guardedly.

"Maybe it's not remote viewing. After all, you told me you have had spontaneous psi experiences since childhood. Perhaps you are uncomfortable with sharing psi with someone else. You may be uncomfortable with me. Maybe you are reluctant to have me evaluate your data and you see me as some sort of a scientific 'judge.' If that's it, I can only hope that will be overcome as we work together on more projects. We do need to evaluate our results carefully, but I don't see myself as an authority. I think of us as coexperimenters, codiscoverers. We are exploring together."

"I understand that," she replied softly. "So how can you explain what happened toward the end of our experiment yesterday?"

"What was that?" I said

"While I was still deeply relaxed, I suddenly saw a man lying down, maybe dead. Then I saw him stand up and come toward me. I thought he was going to attack me—the image was that real. He was at the base of that building. That's what those squiggles mean."

I sat there speechless.

"The terrifying image of that man bothered me all night," she continued. "Was it some suppressed memory, a concern about doing remote viewing…or was it something secret—maybe a warning…about you?"

I had almost forgotten about the incident at the library, but now I clearly understood her dilemma and why she was reluctant to discuss all of her impressions.

"Diane, Diane!" I said with great intensity. "*Congratulations*. You really nailed last night's experience. The target area had more than a library building. You picked up on the entire scene, including the shock I experienced toward the end of the experiment."

She squinted at me. "What do you mean? I'm confused."

"You saw something that happened to me. That 'threatening man' is not a buried memory—and rest assured it is not about me—at least I don't think I look that menacing!"

She grinned.

After I had recounted the story, it was her turn to feel the emotional shockwaves. We sat quietly, staring into our cold coffee.

After a few minutes, she said, "Thank you. Now I know I'm not a crazy woman and that many of my premonitions are not the ramblings of a flake. Psi, as you call it, and this remote viewing, really do work. Thanks for helping me see that."

I explained that sometimes it takes a shocking incident, like that one with the angry man, to make a point. Buildings are great objective targets, but there is a lot more to psi perception than simple forms and shapes. Feelings and emotions are important, too. They fuel the psi process and can come through psi channels loud and clear.

"Diane, we have been here too long. We don't want to upset your supervisor."

"I already have," she replied. "It was his picture that fell off the wall at the moment he made me angry. By the way, thanks for the book *Mental Radio*. Mary Craig Sinclair described childhood experiences similar to mine."

As we left the coffee shop, we quickly made plans for other remote viewing experiments. Maybe our dreams of using remote viewing for helping others, for locating missing pilots or hostages, would not be that far-fetched.

4

Flashing Aircraft

SHORTLY AFTER THAT FIRST VISIT TO SRI, HAL CALLED ME AT MY OFFICE WITH ANOTHER
challenge:

"How would you like to check out remote viewing at two thousand
miles? Late this afternoon I will be visiting a site as a beacon person for
some of our regular remote viewers. Why don't you tag along?"

I was not quite ready for another remote viewing session. The angst
and surprise from my first experience still lingered, and I had mixed feelings concerning the results. Had I just made some lucky guesses? Maybe
the targets hadn't been unique enough and anything I said would have fit
something at or near the site.

Like many people do after experiencing an unusual event that runs
contrary to their prior experience or concepts, I was beginning to feel the
"ink-fish syndrome." British author Arthur Koestler, coined that term to
describe the human tendency to "black out," over time, any experience
that results in cultural dissonance. Eventually we convince ourselves that
the startling experience never took place or that we misinterpreted it.

Gradually I had become surrounded by a crushing octopus of overbear-
ing logic that wanted to strangle my remote viewing experience in inky
blackness. I needed to find a way to keep both mind-partners—my reliable
logical one and my shadowy, hard-to-find, nonlogical, or intuitive, one—in
the same playing field. Neither one should be confined to the penalty box, I
reasoned. To overcome doubts and the butterflies, you go at it again. You
take another look.

"Okay, Hal, you're on," I said. "Why am I such a glutton for punishment?"

"Remote viewing is not punishment," he retorted. "It's supposed to be fun. Looks like you are still struggling with some resistance. Is it the distance? Remember, we have found that distance doesn't affect remote viewing performance. Remember Hella's Cave?"

How could I forget? I could still hear her dramatic description of the Ohio Caverns, and sense her enthusiasm. She certainly had no hang-ups. Why should I?

"No, Hal, it's not the distance," I said. "In fact, that's where the challenge really is. How well can remote viewers do at long distances, even intercontinental?"

"That's one of our most pressing concerns," he answered. "But let's start with baby, continental ones. I know you will enjoy tackling my experiment today. Remember, I can be looking at anything."

The three-hour time difference made it possible for me to try the experiment from the comfort of my basement sanctuary at home. Shortly before 6:00 PM my time, I began the cool-down phase, hoping to achieve a relaxed state by the time Hal arrived at his West Coast target site. I focused on Hal, wondering where he was, what he was looking at. Six o'clock arrived, then six-fifteen, then six-thirty, and the experiment was over. Hal would be leaving the site. I had no image, no perceptions of any kind.

Disappointed, I wondered if I had been thinking too much, wondering where Hal might be. Initially I had had to stifle thoughts of the San Francisco Bay area experiments I had reviewed. Memories of my Inner Quadrangle target intruded. Those nagging doubts and criticisms had taken up their soapbox, too. How could I relax and be open to those faint inner perceptions, right or wrong, when I had orchestrated such inner mental turmoil? Clearly I had not been able to relax and to keep surface consciousness off to the sidelines.

This was also my first solo experiment. As a novice, maybe I needed the presence of a silent coach, an interviewer-helper to crack open my psi gate a little. Was it the confidence Russ had communicated, directly and subliminally? Had I sensed his mental intent for my success at deep levels?

As I pondered these issues, I thought of the objective: *We are trying to determine if remote viewing works, even approximately, at long dis-*

tances. I had felt a need to participate directly in this exploratory process, not remain merely an outside observer. To feel comfortable with results from Hal's regular remote viewers, I had to see for myself. This was my opportunity, and perhaps not many more would come my way. I had to act—now!

Again I tried to relax. The experiment would now be one of retrocognition. I saw nothing wrong with that. We did not understand the remote viewing process, and time seemed quite slippery. Now the gentle query to my subconscious psi gatekeeper was: Where *was* Hal? What *was* he looking at?"

In a few moments, I became drowsy. I had to find that wispy boundary between deep relaxation and sleep. Some remote viewers did not need to be deeply relaxed, but at this time in my inner explorations, I sensed a need to go as deep as possible. I vaguely recall glancing at the clock. It was almost 7:00 PM. I had been waiting, poised for any mentation, any inner perception, for almost one hour, but nothing came.

I was determined to wait until something happened. Earlier I had held strong thoughts of seeing the target area and nothing else. Implicit was the reinforcement to my subconscious to do whatever it could to keep those interfering mind-partners on the sidelines. I reasoned that my unconscious should be able to figure out what was of psi origin and what was not and somehow do the appropriate filtering. I suspected potential distortions occurred after basic psi impressions came through the psi gate, and planned to wrestle with that later.

At 7:15, I drifted into deeper relaxation waiting, keeping thoughts to a minimum. Sometimes my eyes were open, sometimes not.

Then something strange happened. In front of me, before my open eyes, was an exceptionally clear image of what I instantly recognized as some type of airplane. To my amazement, it began to move, drifting from the left. It was very shiny; a large propeller slowly rotated in front of the unusual craft. I could see no wings. It started emitting bright flashes that blocked it momentarily from view. It approached the basement wall on the right and disappeared.

What had I seen? I had been awake, gazing vacantly into dark areas of the basement, when all of a sudden something moved across the room, or seemed to. After regaining my composure, I quickly reasoned that this mind-airplane was internal. My subconscious mind had invested this image with a lot of energy, making it appear to be very real and outside of myself. I could easily have mistaken it for a model airplane.

Now fully alert, I sketched the airplane in as much detail as possible. Since, to date his target pool had only been nice, safe, static scenes in the San Francisco Bay area, I reasoned it could not have been Hal's target. So where had it come from? Was it a hallucination? I had been in session for over an hour. Exhausted, I went to bed early. I was more concerned about that vivid image than I was about missing Hal's target.

For over six years I had kept extensive journals of my important daily activities, unusual experiences, and most dreams. I had read about the successful dream telepathy research at the Maimonides Medical Center in Brooklyn. It occurred to me to try for Hal's target again via a psi dream. Maybe I had sensed where he was during the experimental session, but simply could not pull it to consciousness. What difference did it make if I remote viewed in real time or in past time? What difference did it make if I was relaxed and conscious or asleep? My subconscious mind had to know if I had picked up any relevant impressions. Since I suspected my remote viewing session had failed, I wondered if I could try again in the dream state. Often dreams are filled with memories. Maybe I had a retained subconscious memory of Hal's target that did not surface during my presleep remote viewing attempt. Even if I still missed the target in a dream state, a dream might provide insight into what that strange aircraft image meant. With new dedication, I held focus on dreaming Hal's target right before falling asleep.

I slept soundly. Toward morning, I awoke suddenly and recalled a fleeting dream:

I am walking through a large, open place. It is well main-
tained, something like a memorial garden or park, with
open, grassy areas. I walk toward a small building and

closely observe a large, round design that looks like thick, concentric circles in tan or earth-tone colors.

There was more that I could not recall. I jotted notes on my night pad and crudely sketched the work of art. Shortly after I got up, I recorded the dream in my daily journal.

Then the question: Was this simply a rambling dream that rehashed from memory places I had seen while visiting with Hal, or could it have some relationship, even if inaccurate, to the site Hal had visited?

I slowly drove to the office, trying to keep down new waves of anxiety and doubt about remote viewing and psi. That aircraft image continued to trouble me. At the office, I quickly wrote a note to Hal with a summary of my dream imagery and a copy of my sketch of the round art object, then put them in the morning mail. Around 11:00 AM, I dialed his number.

"Hal," I said impatiently, "I want to apologize right off. I messed up last night and could not relax. Nothing happened that related to your target. I did try again later, hoping for a psi dream." Hal and I had talked about dream-telepathy work, and I knew he was very interested in that form of psi perception.

"That's okay," he said in a reassuring tone. "Psi impressions can occur in many ways, not only remote viewing."

"My dream was brief and only had one clear aspect," I said. After reading my dream summary to him, I waited for his response.

"I don't think you should be disappointed," he said with confidence. "I have a photo I'll send to you. I was walking around in a public recreation area. It was a large park with wide, open lawns and a swimming pool. I had paid close attention to a large coiled rope hanging on the swimming pool building. It reminded me of a Mayan art form."

I was intrigued. Some aspects of his site may have come through, but I still had doubts.

"Maybe my art object correlated, Hal," I said. "But why didn't I sense more of the site? Why didn't I see a swimming pool? Wasn't that the dominant feature?"

"Not necessarily," he replied. "Early on in remote viewing you don't latch onto everything. For some reason, you were more attracted to that large, circular shape. You did have a sense that this was a large, open, parklike area."

"Maybe. But I'm not convinced I did that well."

"This is your first long-distance experiment. And you worked alone. Don't fly before you can walk. Your results were reasonable for a beginner. Based on your impressions, even a tough judge might have selected my park target from other possible targets like a train station, the Hoover Tower, or a marina. Have you forgotten about your Inner Quadrangle?"

I knew he was right. I had to be patient.

"There's something I must tell you," he continued. "While I was at that site, I was distracted and had difficulty getting into the mood of the experiment. I may not have been a good beacon person. Maybe you sensed that. You see, a police helicopter kept circling low overhead, and you know how noisy they are! I couldn't help paying attention to it. I kept wondering if any of the remote viewers sensed my distraction or that heli-copter. But none of them did."

"A *what?*" I could hardly restrain myself.

"A helicopter. Even worse, it kept flashing an intense strobe light. It was blinding to look at!"

My strange, disturbing "image" suddenly made sense. I had latched onto the most interesting—the most emotionally and physically disturb-ing—part of Hal's environment. I was beginning to recognize that, at least for some people, feelings and emotions are more important in the psi process than I had previously suspected. In free-response experiments, our subconscious psi-gatekeeper rules supreme. For me, that unexpected inci-dent was easier to sense during my remote viewing session than the static scene.

When I explained my flashing-aircraft experience, Hal was shocked—and elated.

"We still have a lot to learn." I reminded him. "Apparently, intense feelings and emotions—and images that cause them—can be picked up, even at transcontinental distances."

"That's what the Soviet psi researchers claim," he concurred.

"There is something else, Hal. Remember, I was focusing on what you were *looking at,* what you were *seeing,* not only on what was at the fixed features of the site. So it looks like the way we phrase our objective when we present it to the viewer is very important. We have to be precise in our intent."

"Good point. We have come to accept that as a basic condition. I'm sorry I forgot to tell you," he said, laughing. "The remote viewers of yesterday's project were focused on what geometric features were at the site, not on what I was seeing or experiencing."

We had a long talk about the effect that preferences and cognitive style have on remote viewing perceptions. An artist should do well in describing shapes and geometries. Someone with musical talent should do well in sensing sounds at the target. Our memories and background can also influence our remote viewing perceptions. My airplane-design experience while I was an aeronautical engineer probably influenced the way I perceived the helicopter at Hal's site, and I subconsciously added a front-end propeller to the basic remote viewing image.

Before we signed off, I said, "Thanks, Hal. Thanks for choosing a great site." We laughed.

The light that flashed at Hal's target let me glimpse more clearly the vast range of our subconscious reach. Maybe we are all like beacons, signaling out at all times to those who are receptive.

5

Where Is She?

HELLA AND DIANE HAD SHOWN ME THAT ACCURATE INFORMATION CAN INDEED COME from our remote viewing potential. My Flashing Aircraft experience was another reminder that we can reach out across thousands of miles and perceive the environment surrounding others. Now I was wrestling with just what could be done with that information?

If our psi potential is a neutral phenomena that is accessible to all, then, like our other senses, it must have helped our early ancestors during their touch-and-go struggle for survival. Anthropologists have documented accounts of some aboriginal people who still rely on ESP to locate animals or other food sources. How can psi help us today?

A straightforward remote viewing application was apparent: to find missing or lost items, missing or lost people. Certainly there were other possibilities. I planned to explore many of them in time.

I imagined exercises in "finding things." Could remote viewing impressions be accurate enough for locating someone? Had I been held captive near or in a building that looked like Diane's sketch of the Dayton Library, could I have been found? Had a child stumbled down an overgrown sinkhole, into a cave, would remote viewing data like Hella provided for the Ohio Caverns have helped the search team? Would my vivid Flashing Aircraft image have provided a clue for locating a hostage held near a helicopter landing strip?

Experiments like these and many others showed that remote viewing could help in identifying general search areas. Remote viewing had practical utility for search-and-rescue missions, depending on circumstances.

What about applying remote viewing to finding things in my own life? Were results of my first visit to SRI nothing more than a fluke? Could

Flashing Aircraft or the psi dreams I occasionally had be repeated? The only way to find out was simply to take a look—do remote viewing; explore. Once I had decided to try remote viewing the next time finding needs entered my own life, I did not have long to wait.

A family situation developed that required my wife Barbara and I to travel to Hamburg, our hometown in eastern Pennsylvania, five hundred miles from Dayton. Business commitments made it necessary for me to drive there on my own from Washington, D.C., which is two hundred miles south of the town. I planned to arrive at my parents' house early that Friday evening, while Barbara was to leave Dayton late Thursday night, which would bring her to my parents' home early Friday afternoon. When I arrived that evening, she had yet to arrive. I suspected she had not left as early as planned, and was running a few hours late.

By 9:00 PM, I'd had no word from Barbara. It was March. The sky was clear. The weather conditions through the Pennsylvania mountains could be unpredictable at that time of year, though no late-winter storms had been forecast.

At 10:00, with no word still, I thought it strange that she had not called with an update on her time of arrival. Maybe the car experienced mechanical difficulty somewhere along the route. Did she have my parents' phone number? Perhaps she was stranded some distance from a phone....

When it got to be 11:00 PM, my old friend anxiety crept from his nearby lair and pushed my calmer self aside. I paced. Occasionally, with my face pressed against the kitchen window, I watched headlights pass the exit to Hamburg. Not many cars turned off.

In my mind, I ran through things I could do. I could call the state police. I had already called our home in Dayton, but there had been no answer. I knew she had left, but when? Where was she now?

I thought about the "finding" scenarios I had imagined so often. Here I was, rapidly disintegrating into basket-case condition—how could anyone do remote viewing at a time like this? But what else could I do? I wasn't ready to call anyone for help or to send out a search party.

I curled up in a comfortable chair in the darkened living room and tried to hold my focus:

Where Is Barbara?

Trying to relax and let the images flow, only my overactive imagination responded. Maybe I could doze and try later.

Around 11:30 I went to bed and, surprisingly, quickly fell asleep. I woke around midnight, feeling refreshed. Remaining in bed, I once again held my focus:

Where Is Barbara?

In a few moments, a vivid image appeared. At first it appeared as a vague form, like a darkened hole or tunnel, then I perceived curving white bands that twisted and turned. A darkened scene, something like a mountain area, flashed briefly. That was all. I had no sense of difficulty of any kind.

If the image related in any way to her whereabouts, only one possibility came to mind: The twisting, S-curves at the exit from the Allegheny Mountain tunnel on the Pennsylvania Turnpike. If Barbara were there, I could fairly reliably predict that she would arrive in three hours. Since I felt no sense of foreboding, I was reasonably sure she was not stranded somewhere. Whether by rationale or an inner knowledge, I quickly fell asleep. I woke shortly before 3:00 AM—about a minute before the car pulled into the driveway.

Shortly after we moved to Prince Frederick, Maryland, Barbara had taken a long business trip. It was winter and the weather was unpredictable. Although she set out in good weather, conditions turned bad the day of her return.

I was waiting at National Airport for her flight from St. Louis. It arrived around 9:00 PM as expected, but Barbara was not on-board. Since there was no message anywhere, I assumed her connecting flight to St. Louis was delayed and that she had had to hustle to arrange for a new booking. The schedule showed several more flights due to arrive from St. Louis, Chicago, and other Midwestern airports. Perhaps she'd caught one of them. If not, I was sure she would have the airline page me with a message.

Anxiously, I loitered near the baggage area as the remaining flights landed. Barbara was not on board any of them. A few flights were delayed, and I waited for them. No Barbara. Only a delayed flight from Atlanta was shown, now scheduled for 1:00 AM, but I could not see how that could figure into any impromptu connections. I had no choice but to drive the sixty miles home and wait for her call. I left before the flight from Atlanta arrived.

I began the long drive home, exhausted and a bit anxious. Where was Barbara stuck for the night? Was she alright? As I began to relax and unwind, I found myself wondering uneasily if she had caught that flight from Atlanta. Had I left her stranded at National Airport?

Shortly after I arrived home, I focused on:

Where Is Barbara?

As I was about to drift asleep, an image flashed in my mind: It looked like a well-designed, high-rise hotel. It was taller than any building I would have expected her to be in, had she been unable to leave the area she was visiting. Maybe it was wishful thinking. The image did invoke a sense of peace and I felt that wherever she was, all was well. If that impression was on track, then at least she was not stuck in an airport somewhere. Later that night, I had several brief dreams with a motif of a modern hotel that reminded me of a Ramada Inn or a Holiday Inn.

Early the next morning I received a message from her at my office. She *had* been on that flight from Atlanta! Creative rerouting brought her to Atlanta in time to catch that delayed flight but there had been no time to call and leave a message. When she arrived at a by-then deserted National Airport, all she could do was take a taxi to a nearby hotel—the Holiday Inn. She had tried to call me, but I was still en route home. Exhausted, she fell asleep.

We had our answering machine repaired after that incident.

I should have tried to locate her via remote viewing while I was at the airport. An image of an airplane from an Southern location could have come to mind. That sudden gut feeling about leaving Barbara stranded at National Airport makes me suspect I knew at some level that she was on the Atlanta flight. I had allowed my rational mind to get in the way.

The next time I am waiting in an airport for someone who is delayed, I will find a quiet, darkened corner in a lounge and ask my remote viewing tracker the question: "Where Is She?"

6

Arctic Search

IN THE MID-1970S, THE PHYSICS DEPARTMENT AT DREXEL UNIVERSITY IN PHILADELPHIA sponsored a meeting on consciousness and psi research. At this conference, I had a lengthy discussion with Ed Mitchell, the former astronaut. My earlier responsibilities as an aeronautical engineer on the Gemini space program prompted a strong interest in NASA's space activities. Ed told me of his unofficial ESP test during the Apollo 14 moon-landing mission in 1971. I was amazed that anyone, especially a hard-nosed, nuts-and-bolts astronaut who had training in science would even consider participating in such an experiment. He was interested in the communication potential of ESP for space missions.

During the Apollo 14 mission, for his ESP experiment Ed set aside a seven-minute period when no other activity was planned. During this time—twice en route to the moon, and twice on the return—he randomly selected twenty-five ESP-testing symbols like those initially used by J. B. Rhine. These were either a star, cross, wavy line, circle, or square. After each selection, Ed focused attention on that symbol for fifteen seconds, and on the four participants on Earth, two hundred thousand miles away. At a prearranged time, his fellow experimenters on Earth focused on perceiving the symbols on which Ed was concentrating. Their impressions were dated and recorded.

Shortly after Ed's return to Earth, his records and the impressions of the four participants were provided for analysis to Dr. Rhine's laboratory, which is now the Rhine Research Center in Durham, North Carolina. Dr. Karlis Osis at the American Society for Psychical Research in New York City performed additional analysis. Results were statistically significant, suggesting that a psi link had occurred. The press sensationalized the experiments, much to the embarrassment of NASA officials, who had not been aware of Ed's project. However, Dr. Werner von Braun, noted rocket scientist, was intrigued and felt the phenomenon should be examined systematically.

As I listened to Ed, my own vision of exploring psi's communication potential became stronger. Fixed symbols or numbers seemed too limiting for practical applications. Laboratory experiments yielded low reliability when they were used as psi targets. However, psi research at the Maimonides Medical Center had shown that the transfer of pictorial information frequently could succeed. At this time, remote viewing at SRI was only beginning, and I had not seen any of their experimental results. I wondered if a remote scene could be sensed reliably by a psi sensitive. If people could describe remote scenes as accurately as nearby pictures, then I could see the potential for tracking people who were traveling, or lost. I considered psi tracking as one-way communication—the traveler communicates via psi his or her location to another, distant person.

Ed Mitchell may have sensed my keen interest in his ESP experiment and in the communication possibilities of psi. As we talked, he told me about a long-distance, Arctic psi tracking experiment. It was the type of project I had been considering. My interest in white-water canoeing had escalated over the years and I had recently gone on long river journeys in the Canadian far north. During these trips, I had often wondered if anyone with psi talent could tune in to us and tell how we were progressing, or sense that we needed help in an emergency.

Ed Mitchell's account of the Sir Hubert Wilkins–Harold Sherman ESP experiment during a hazardous search mission in the Arctic rekindled my interest in psi tracking. Although their adventure occurred during the fall and winder of 1937–38, it invoked within me a spirit of exploration that felt timeless. Shortly after that conference I obtained a copy of their book, *Thoughts Through Space*, first published in 1941, and read it thoroughly.

Sir Hubert Wilkins, the noted British aviator and Arctic explorer, had been knighted for his pioneering use of airplanes for Arctic exploration and for demonstrating their utility under winter conditions. Harold Sherman was a professional writer and a noted psychic sensitive who lived in New York City. Sir Hubert and Harold met frequently at the Explorers Club in New York.

In the summer of 1937, the Soviet Union began exploratory flights over the polar regions to study the feasibility of a new commercial air route between Europe and North America. Their first two flights between Moscow and Fairbanks, Alaska, were successful. The third one, piloted by Sigismund Levanevsky, with a crew of five, disappeared somewhere in the Arctic. The Russians initiated a massive search. After a few months, Levanevsky had not been found. As the winter months, with the specter of continuous darkness, approached, search activities were suspended.

Russian authorities were aware of Sir Hubert's Arctic winter-flying experience and asked him to continue the search through the winter if necessary. He accepted this challenging mission. In a few weeks, he began search flights from Aklavik, a small Inuit village located where the Mackenzie River spills into the Arctic Ocean. Sir Hubert continued flying search missions for six months. He could not find Levanevsky's plane, and it is still missing, probably covered by snow or submerged deep in icy water.

Before Sir Hubert left the United States with his small team, he met Harold Sherman for lunch at the Explorers Club. He told Harold that he was concerned that radio equipment was not adequate for operating under Arctic winter conditions. Should he come down on Arctic ice, bad weather or equipment unreliability could make contact with a rescue team impossible. Harold suggested they try to establish contact via ESP as a possible communication back-up should he become missing. The idea intrigued Sir Hubert.

The explorer had frequently experienced unusual coincidences that he felt could not be due to chance. When living in Australia, he had observed evidence of ESP among aborigines. He had often wondered if someone with ESP ability could provide information accurately enough for his rescue should he become stranded in an isolated location. They both considered Sir Hubert's Arctic search mission an excellent opportunity for testing the potential of ESP for search-and-rescue.

Harold set aside a one-hour period three times a week during which he relaxed and sought ESP impressions of what Sir Hubert was experiencing at around the same time. They also set up a few experiments with ESP testing cards. During Harold's session, Sir Hubert reviewed events he had recorded in a journal and focused attention on Harold, hoping he would perceive those thoughts. Immediately after each session, Harold sent copies of his impressions to Dr. Gardner Murphy, a well-known psychologist at Columbia University. Dr. Murphy verified their dates, kept them on file, and helped in their evaluation when Sir Hubert's real experiences became known.

During these evening sessions, Harold perceived specific incidents when they occurred—accidents, unexpected changes in plans, equipment failures, injuries, and a village fire. His impressions of many routine events correlated to real events. Harold's attempt to sense ESP-card symbols had a small degree of success. He felt such targets lacked emotional intensity or interest, both conditions he felt to be vital for ESP communication.

Harold had little difficulty sensing when Sir Hubert was flying long missions. A few of them—nearly twenty-four hours at a stretch—pushed Sir Hubert's endurance to the limit. Sir Hubert's emotional intensity during these long flights and when crises occurred seemed like a beacon to Harold. Occasionally Sir Hubert was temporarily isolated with an inoperative radio and had no conventional way of communicating with team members in Aklavik. Harold's impressions during these periods could have been of potential help had Sir Hubert remained isolated.

Although Harold did not sense all the important situations, or was off concerning the time of their occurrence, his overall success rate was sufficient to demonstrate that psi had application potential for search-and-rescue missions.

I set aside *Thoughts Through Space*, wondering how, even in some small way, I might replicate this pioneering effort. An idea came to me. If Harold Sherman or Sir Hubert were still alive, perhaps I could meet with them and learn more about their experiment. I discovered that Sir Hubert had died in 1958 but Harold Sherman, now seventy-eight years old, was living in Mountain View, Arkansas, where he continued to investigate and write about psi phenomena.

Not long after that fortuitous discussion with Ed Mitchell, I became directly involved in the remote viewing research at SRI. My first get-acquainted trip to their laboratory in Menlo Park brought a pleasant surprise: Harold Sherman was there! He dropped by occasionally to visit Hal Puthoff. Shortly after meeting him, I brought up *Thoughts Through Space* and we had a very long discussion about that milestone experiment.

I felt comfortable with Harold, and could see why he leaned toward the mind contact or telepathy—rather than the neutral, form-structure—remote viewing mode for psi impressions. He believed that emotional connections with people were essential for good psi contact. This seemed to be more of a mind-to-mind situation than remote viewing of the environment. It was apparent that Harold's rapport with Sir Hubert was the essential ingredient for the success he achieved during their marathon psi communication project.

That evening during dinner together I raised an interesting idea that had occurred to me earlier, but I had dismissed at the time. As we talked, however, I sensed that Harold would be open to my request.

"Harold," I said, cautiously, "I want to tell you how important your courageous experiment is to me. You did what I have only recently envisioned: psi communication from thousands of miles away with explorers or travelers in remote areas, like the Antarctic or Arctic regions. I have been considering a long-distance psi experiment in the Arctic, but have not yet approached anyone about participating in it. It occurred to me that you might, after almost forty years, like to revisit the Arctic."

I wondered if Harold sensed the drift of my conversation—and how he would react when he heard my question.

He was listening intently.

"You see, one of my hobbies, you might call it an obsession, is whitewater canoeing. I have planned and participated in canoe races and have traveled across thousands of miles of the great Canadian rivers by canoe. Each year, I join other members of our small canoe club, The Voyagers Canoe Club of North America, to travel farther and farther north. This year, in July, we plan to tackle the remote Coppermine River in Canada's Northwest Territories and will be on the river three weeks or longer.

He said nothing.

"How would you like to travel along and keep track of us on this journey, while you are comfortably at home, like you did with Sir Hubert?"

To my surprise, his response was immediate. "I would love to return to the Arctic! I haven't taken part in a long-distance experiment for some time and I would like to see the Arctic again. Yes, yes, that's a great idea!"

Encouraged by his enthusiastic acceptance, I began initial plans for our experiment. Harold agreed to the timing and documentation requirements: He would set aside a one-hour period, three times a week, during which he would attempt to perceive impressions of our journey. They could be highlights of activities, incidents, unique features of the terrain, or whatever came to him. I would keep a detailed journal, take photographs, and make movies. He would have his data notarized and mailed to Hal Puthoff. Upon my return, several people and I would compare actual events with his notarized data. While we knew this could not be considered a scientific experiment, I felt I could gain valuable insight into psi's communication and search potential.

The weeks passed quickly as six of us—three experienced adults and three teenage novices—prepared for our forthcoming journey. Planning and logistics, equipment purchases and repairs filled our spare time. In late July we were finally ready to leave. I placed a call to Harold who was as excited about our upcoming adventure as we were.

We departed Dayton and drove to Yellowknife, capital of Canada's Northwest Territories, where we loaded our gear and canoes into a large floatplane and took off for Lac de Gras, source of the Coppermine River deep in the Arctic tundra. After a few hours, the bush pilot descended and skimmed onto the lake. Spray erupted and drenched the windshield; propellers whined in reverse thrust. The pilot cut power and we drifted onto a sandy beach. Around us spread the beauty of a primitive tundra wilderness—flowering plants, Arctic wildlife, constant daylight.

After unloading our gear, the plane roared away, blasting spray. It snapped into the sky and slowly faded from sight. We were alone, isolated from civilization. Quickly we loaded our canoes, tightened waterproof decking, and started off downstream. The river would drop a total of 1,400 feet as it made its way to the Arctic Ocean, 400 miles north.

Our journey had begun.

Early in the journey, I wrote:

```
Today Chris [one of the teenagers] is very sick from black-
fly bites. His face is puffed up, his eyelids are nearly
swollen shut, and he has difficulty breathing. It looks
like we might have to hold up a day or two for him to
recover.
```

At that time, Harold, who was some two thousand miles to the southeast, sensed that someone was sick, and wrote:

```
Does someone have a cold or hay fever—sinus difficulties?
```

One day, as we approached the Arctic Circle, we paddled toward a low, hazy, overcast horizon. It was not mist or fog, but dense, choking smoke from a nearby tundra fire! Our eyes burned, we choked and coughed, barely able to breathe. I was beginning to feel dizzy and had trouble balancing the canoe. Later that day, the wind shifted. By the next day, only a slight haze remained.

We camped early the following day at the base of a large esker (a sand-gravel ridge) where I caught up on my journal writing.

That night Harold recorded:

```
I see Dale working on his diary. There is a slope behind
him rising to a clifflike background....The atmosphere is
very hazy.
```

The journey required us to make a few portages. With careful reconnoitering, our decking tightly lashed over the canoes, we were able to navigate most of the rapids. Late one day, completely exhausted after struggling against a strong headwind, we came to Obstruction Rapids. We thought it best to portage around the raging white-water. In the morning, we carried our canoes a half-mile over rocks and through brush to a calm bay below the rapids. The next day, Harold wrote in his journal:

Camped yesterday before a waterfall which required a portage. They decided to do this portage in the morning when everyone was fresh, to make a carry of an eighth of a mile.

We did not expect to meet anyone on this journey—there were no settlements or outposts—yet one day we had a surprise encounter with two people, who came to us by motorboat from a small camp on the right shoreline. They were geologists in the region for the summer. During our brief chat, they warned us of the grizzlies ahead. That evening, Harold wrote:

Is it possible Dale and his party have had a surprise encounter with two natives on the right side of the river? Prospectors? They warn of treacherous rapids ahead.

On another evening, we camped near the beginning of the major rapids. Scouting ahead on land, we felt we could run the rapids successfully. Beyond them loomed Rocky Defile, a deep canyon filled with thundering rapids. That evening we talked until late about the difficult days ahead, aware that years earlier canoeists had capsized and drowned in this region. Below Rocky Defile, the turbulence of Hell's Gate and the plunge at Bloody Falls waited for us. We all felt tense, uncertain of what might happen. My canoe partner was my son, Dale, Jr. (Bud), whom I suspected also felt uneasy. This river was his first major white-water challenge.

I felt more apprehension than the others. Sick from eating unripe berries and from numerous black-fly bites, my strength was at a low level and my sense of balance was affected. Our campsite that evening was close to an old burial site that Chuck, Fred, and I found while searching for bearberries. It was a large formation of rocks in the size and shape of a burial mound. A dozen thin wooden poles with pointed ends protruded from the stones. They were tilted at an angle, as if to discourage grizzlies from climbing up. We could find no names carved on any of these weather-beaten poles. Lichens covered most of the rocks, which indicated that the burial occurred over one hundred years earlier. The grave could not be very deep, since permafrost was only a few inches below the sphagnum moss that blanketed this region of the river valley.

Around our campfire that night we wondered what had happened to that early traveler. Did he or she die of an illness, or was it starvation? Could death have resulted from a grizzly bear attack, or from hypothermia due to a capsize in the frigid Coppermine River? I frequently glanced toward the grove of stunted spruce that provided some protection for the grave, wondering about the drama that occurred here many years ago. Being in such close proximity to that grave added to my angst.

That night, I had a nightmare: In it I am in an ambulance, being rushed to a hospital dying. The ambulance crashes....I awoke from the nightmare, sick and troubled. Was something terribly wrong with me? Was I in danger of dying? Was that a precognitive warning of being dashed on the jagged rocks by the raging white-water ahead?

With great reluctance, I slipped out of my sleeping bag and began the day. Excitement of being in rapids and the challenge of a difficult run helped me recover, or forget, my illness. The first rapids, a half-mile long, were almost a disaster. I misread the current and came very close to capsizing in the surging, icy water. The river was full of sharp boulders that caused the current to swirl, creating hydraulics and whirlpools. We were drawn into a huge wave—a haystack—that ripped off our decking. Water poured in. I shouted to Bud to get to shore. With intense effort, we made it to the right side, but had great difficulty pulling the water-filled canoe out of the swift current. I had to jump out of the canoe in waist-deep water to push it to safety. The sequence was captured on film.

I felt much better that evening but was still puzzled by that nightmare. Had my weakened condition, and angst, been the cause? Had my illness, my high anxiety about the dangerous rapids, affected Harold in any way?

Around the time I became sick and had my nightmare, Harold woke up from a disturbing dream at 5:00 AM:

I am troubled in my sleep tonight....My conscious mind does not want to let me think something tragic has happened, but I feel helpless to do anything about it.

For the first time, I see canoes swirling out of control....men struggling in the water....fighting for their lives. I hope this is only a dramatization of my concern rather than a real occurrence....a reflection of the actual fear present in the minds of Dale and others. Can helicopters be sent to check?

I am experiencing the same emotional disturbance I underwent several times in the Sir Hubert experiments so many years ago, when I felt his life to have been in peril...later proven correct.

I am impressed to record these thoughts as I try to free my mind from its concern for Dale and his party, and to make an objective evaluation of the real condition existing.

The previous day he had written:

This river venture is developing into quite a saga....I can feel emotional excitement mounting. New hazards are encountered which are challenging the skill and endurance of the canoeists....The river runs wild, twisting and turning. Anxious moments today approaching a narrow channel bounded by rock formations—a stretch of perhaps a half-mile. Suddenly they were almost sucked into the rapids....I feel a possible turnover....Getting to shore is not easy....I seem to be on the right side of the river, they have just escaped a possible catastrophe....Timing is difficult....The events may be coming toward them....Tonight I feel like I had been hit in the solar plexus.

Harold's impressions of a possible river tragedy prompted him to contact Hal Puthoff at SRI. To Harold, it seemed that I and the canoe party needed immediate help. Should a search-and-rescue team be sent in? Harold was confident in his impressions, but he could not be sure of the boundary between literal and symbolic elements. Had his subconscious mind embellished or colored the basic impressions, or did we really need to be rescued—immediately? He knew there was no way we could get help in this remote, isolated region of the Arctic. We had no emergency radio transmitter.

Hal acknowledged Harold's concern, but recommended a cautious approach and suggested a day's delay before taking any action. Harold accepted Hal's advice to hold off on initiating a search. The following day he sought to detect our current status, to see if we still needed help. To his surprise, he sensed a peaceful camp scene and felt that all was well. He wrote:

I feel relieved, as though some possible crisis which could have triggered my deep concern, has been passed or surmounted.

He slept well that night.

Several days later, the weather pattern shifted; low clouds portended rain. We had an early lunch on a wide, rocky part of the river's flood plain. A light drizzle misted the air. After having soup and sandwiches, we all stood around near the canoes, talking and relaxing. Something under the low black spruce trees that filled this section of the river valley caught my attention. Beneath its branches, I saw a bird—an Arctic tern. As I gazed at the tern, a soft, gentle feeling, a warm glow, gradually crept through me. I sensed a profound connection to that bird, and to the primeval setting. Something like a feeling of beauty, of deep attunement with nature swept through me.

Not knowing why, I felt the urge to quietly say: "Arctic tern, you are a beautiful bird." Suddenly the tern flew up from the protection of the spruce trees, flew toward me, swooped down, and landed on my head! We all were amazed. My companions recorded it on movie film.

When the drizzle turned to rain, I shooed the tern away so I could put on my hooded rain jacket. To my delight, the tern came back and, once again, landed on my head. It remained seated there, even when I walked around. When we resumed our paddling, the bird followed us downriver, sometimes diving low over our canoe, sometimes hovering above us. As the rain increased, it flew away to shelter under the thick spruce trees on the nearby shore.

During that time, an impression came to Harold that we were giving unusual attention to birds.

```
I see a large, hawklike bird swooping down....
```

Toward the end of our long river journey, both the weather and the river turned ferocious. Heavy rain pounded us. The boulder-filled river surged and heaved, twisting between the narrow canyon walls below Hell's Gate. Once in the canyon, we were committed to the river—no portaging up the 200-foot-high, vertical cliffs was possible. Rain streaked and fogged my glasses; mist shrouded the canyon. Brian and Chuck were in the lead canoe, but I could not see them or the channel they found. The roar from cascading current blocked our paddling-instruction shouts.

Angry waves pounded and rocked the canoe, hurling icy spray into my face. I forced the paddle hard, pulling deep, powerful strokes to twist and turn the canoe in split-second maneuvers. Bud and I struggled along, keeping balance, finding safe channels. Our paddling became synchronized; we were totally focused on the churning, foaming water. The rapids seemed to have no end. We had no choice but to keep plunging ahead.

Our waterproof rain gear could not hold back the drenching rain indefinitely. Strong wind raced up the canyon, forcing our canoes off course. Exhausted and chilled, we had to get to shore. Backpaddling hard, we maneuvered into a small cove. On a ledge, we set up a tarp at the mouth of a small cave. We struggled against buffeting gusts to secure our tents on the narrow rocky ledge. The rain increased, a tundra storm moved in, lightning flashed, thunder cracked, cold rain drenched the treeless tundra above. Water poured from the cliff and crashed against the rocks below. White spray bounced high against the canyon wall. I was too exhausted to write a long account of the day's adventure in my journal.

Before entering my tent, I gazed around this primitive, turbulent scene. Something tugged at my soul—something ancient, timeless. Words from Coleridge's "Kubla Khan" came to mind: "Through caverns measureless by man, down to a sunless sea." On that ledge high above the canyon, something—another immeasurable canyon?—resonated deep within me. As I slipped into my cozy sleeping bag, I thought about Harold. I could almost see him. Drifting off to sleep, I kept wondering if Harold had sensed today's drama. Around that time, he wrote:

```
Landscape is changing, it is more barren, desolate, with
solid rock formations, jagged rocks, little or no vegeta-
tion, few trees. The river rushes through canyons with sud-
den twists and turns, a windy day and choppy water. They
have run into dense fog and rain which has caused them to
wait it out....
    A severe electrical, wind, and rain storm drove them off
the river. I see torrents of rain. Water is cascading over
and down rock canyons and mountainsides....They head toward
a protective cove....They have erected a makeshift covering
of some kind...on a ledgelike formation looking out over the
river....They have encountered more strenuous and hazardous
experiences than they had counted on!
```

We arose energized the next day and continued our river saga. After portaging around Bloody Falls, on the final paddle into the village of Coppermine on the Arctic Ocean, we struggled in dense fog against strong tidal currents and ocean swells. When the fog lifted, we could see icebergs off-shore. We had reached the Arctic Ocean.

A week later, back in Dayton, I received a copy of Harold's journal with his impressions. I felt as if I was reading from my journal! Many of his impressions correlated to unique incidents that could not have been guessed.

When I called him, I could tell he had enjoyed the journey as much as we had. Except, that is, for the time when he felt that something tragic had happened. After I told him about my apprehension, illness, and nightmare, he could understand why he felt that something catastrophic had already happened. During his ESP experiment with Sir Hubert, he had frequently picked up Sir Hubert's concern about an upcoming mission, even when the mission was unexpectedly delayed. Harold came to believe that a memory of a real event or the anticipation of a possible future one—especially if it was emotionally intense—look the same to our psi sensitivities.

It was clear to me that Harold could connect with people at emotional levels. He could feel what they did and relive their experiences no matter how far away they were. I wondered if his deep concern for me and my companions represented more than a one-way communication from me to him. Through our subconscious connection, had he helped me avoid a possible disastrous situation? Maybe I recovered from my illness more quickly than I would have otherwise. Maybe I was better able to navigate treacherous rapids when my performance was off due to illness. I will never know.

Many of his impressions were of routine occurrences, and such observations could not make a case for psi contact. However, others were unique enough to indicate that Harold had somehow joined us on our wilderness adventure. He was able to reexperience his earlier Arctic experiment, I believe, more vividly than he had expected.

An unusual incident that occurred six months after our Coppermine River experiment gave me additional confidence that Harold had made, and was still keeping, psi contact with me. Fortunately, the event was not as critical as those he had experienced with Sir Hubert.

When I first met Harold, he had told me about spontaneous psi experiences with Sir Hubert Wilkins after their experiment. On several occasions Harold perceived incidents that he later found had happened. One day Harold perceived Sir Hubert surrounded by smoke and fire. That same day, Sir Hubert had come close to being seriously burned or even killed when an experiment he was conducting with fireproof gear went out of control. Another time, Harold perceived Sir Hubert receiving a shoulder injury in a serious accident on the very day when he was in a bus that crashed. Several people had been killed, including the person to whom he had earlier given his seat. Sir Hubert suffered a broken collarbone and an injured arm.

Harold's psi connection with me continued, as I discovered when teaching "The Psychic Realm," which I developed after my return from the Coppermine River. As part of the course, I gave class members the opportunity to take part in psi experiments. Some of them only wanted to study the topic; others wanted to see if they had psi talent. For the first experiment, I selected as a "target" an interesting art print with little inherent emotional content, hoping that class members could detect it's basic elements. That night I had a horrific nightmare involving a violent scene filled with fear and destruction. Several elements of the dream were surreal, which was highly unusual for my dream content. I woke up feeling terrible and could not imagine why I had such a troubling dream.

To my surprise, Harold Sherman called me the next morning. I had not talked to him for five months. During the night he "had a vivid impression of me in some tragic situation...maybe a bad accident." He was relieved to learn I was well and had not been in an accident. He wasn't sure why, but felt that I should be extra careful that week. Though he did not say so, I suspected he had a feeling that something tragic was coming my way.

As I described my dream, we realized there were similarities between it and the nightmare I had had during the Coppermine River journey. For some reason I had brought that old material back to surface. Even though he was relieved to learn that my tragic experience had been only in a nightmare, I could sense his concern. Maybe a difficult situation was approaching. I planned to be extra careful.

Later that week, I learned that Harold's concern was on track, at least partially. Something troubling did come my way.

A few days after my nightmare, I began receiving the letters I had requested my class members to mail me. Sending in their impressions of my psi target was good for recordkeeping and also facilitated their discussion in the next class. As the letters came in, I was pleased to see that a few people had done well.

Later that week I received a letter from Beverly, one of the class members, with a detailed description of a nightmare she had had the same night I had mine. Her nightmare had fear and devastation themes similar to mine. It looked like we had a shared nightmare! The dream had no obvious connection to current concerns or events in my life and no association to my psi target. I suspected my nightmare may have been caused by

Beverly's dream experience. I had felt a rapport building with class members, and Harold Sherman had shown me how emotions can flash like powerful beacons in the psi domain. When we discussed her dream after the next class, she could think of no cause for it. She said there were no concerns in her life at that time.

Later, I reexamined the contents of our nightmares from a literal and symbolic point of view. Since my nightmare had self-destructive and surreal aspects, and hers had elements that made me think of associations to drugs, I made the tentative assumption that a serious physical or psychological problem may be coming her way. I planned to talk with her personally after the next class.

During our private discussion, I could find no obvious cause for the devastating nightmare. Although she had been experiencing minor physical discomforts, they did not seem to be significant enough to generate this nightmare. I recommended that she have a physical check-up, which she scheduled.

Weeks later, after the physical, she called me with news of the findings. Traces of a powerful, medically prescribed drug were still in her system. After years of dominance, it was now causing the minor ailments she had been experiencing. The drug, once used during pregnancy, generated serious side effects, and was eventually barred from further use. Fortunately, there were ways of treating the condition. Her dream, and possibly mine, had functioned as a medical alert that had come at an opportune moment. Although she hadn't been successful in identifying my target picture, in opening up her sensitivities she had detected something far more important.

In the space of just a few months, I had made initial explorations into the communication and search potential of psi. Clearly the two main types of psi data—the visualized data of remote viewing, and the sense information from telepathy or feeling—had potential for helping others, even for saving lives. I learned from Harold Sherman and from Beverly that our thoughts can reach out and be heard in time of need.

Icy Arctic rivers had whispered, "exploration." Now currents from deep within my psyche were calling.

Tracking psi in
the Dreamscape

Dream telepathy, dealing with the individual's efforts to
make contact with distant reality and with the social
nature of man's unconscious powers, is likely to be among
the sparks which will be made into a science within the
next century. We cannot afford to ignore such sparks.

➤ Gardner Murphy, Foreword to Ullman, Krippner, and Vaughan's
Dream Telepathy (page xiii)

n 1952, researchers at the University of Chicago, who were monitoring eye motions on subjects sleeping in a laboratory setting, observed throughout the night frequent periods of rapid-eye movement (REM). When awakened right after these REM cycles, the subject recalled the dreams even though the individual may have had very little previous dream recall. Brain wave activity during REM periods resembled the awake state. Further dream-cycle studies showed that most people dream at least six to eight times a night. Our initial dreams are usually brief; toward morning they can be sixty to ninety minutes in length.

Dreams are part of our ancient heritage. Dream content was considered important by aboriginal societies and early civilizations. Australian bushmen still observe dreamtime for receiving information about the state of health of distant relatives or the approach of unexpected travelers. Ruling classes in early Middle Eastern and Egyptian societies relied on dreams for insight. Early Greeks built hundreds of temples where healing dreams could be experienced. Japan and other Asian cultures had similar temples. The dream state as a source for healing and gaining otherwise inaccessible information has historically been part of shamanistic belief worldwide. During the Middle Ages in Europe, dreams were feared and considered by many to come from some evil origin. The role of dreams fell into further decline and essentially vanished in those societies where industrialization and rationalistic philosophies became dominant. It is understandable that our modern society, with its emphasis of empirical science and roots in European culture, generally disregards, even ridicules, the content of dreams. Prior to the discovery of the rapid-eye-movement (REM) dream cycle in 1952, most people assumed a dream state rarely occurred. When dreams were remembered, they were considered to be "only a dream," implying a useless fantasy.

Electroencephalograph (EEG) equipment, first developed early in this century, along with modern data processing systems, have made it possible to monitor brain activity. The electrical patterns, or brain waves, from EEG measurements have opened a new window of understanding for some aspects of our conscious and unconscious mental processes. Over the past several decades, many studies have examined the physiology of sleep and dreaming. Sleep clinics focusing on sleep disorders are becoming part of up-to-date medical centers.

Dream-state research has shown that dreams are vital for health and wellness. When deprived of our dream cycle, we experience a variety of physical and psychological difficulties. Continuous use of certain drugs or alcohol can disrupt our REM cycle, which, in turn, can lead to serious sleep disorders.

While our physiology during dreaming is important from a medical point of view, a variety of opinions exist about the importance of dream content. Some researchers believe the EEG patterns during dreams reflect only random patterns and that dream material, if not meaningless, only represents a routine processing of memories of daily events.

Many individuals who explore their dreams have discovered that dream material can be meaningful. The benchmarks for the rediscovery of dream-content importance begin in the late 1800s and early 1900s, when psychiatrists Sigmund Freud and Carl Jung published their findings on the significance of dreams. Freud saw dream content as representing unresolved suppressed material. Jung saw it as representing the dreamer's unconscious desire for self-discovery and achieving a sense of completeness or wholeness. The works of Freud and Jung reopened a window into our subconscious that had been closed—slammed shut—centuries earlier in Western culture.

Those who work with dreams have found that dream content is influenced by our attitudes toward dreaming. Our subconscious mind can give us dreams that provide us with insight for problem solving and relationship issues. Dreams can be the source of new ideas. Many creative people, such as writers, artists, and inventors, rely on dream-state material for inspiration: Thomas Edison used catnaps for insight; Robert Louis Stevenson's novels originated with dreams; and Albert Einstein had childhood dreams that called attention to relative motion and motivated him to pursue work that led to his relativity and gravitational theories.

Psi researchers and practitioners find that some degree of relaxation that minimizes interference from our conscious thoughts is necessary to their work. Since dreams occur during a naturally relaxing sleep state, it is logical to expect dreams to be a productive means to experience parapsychological phenomena.

In fact, many people do report dreams that they later discover to have had psi elements. Between 1930 and 1960, Louisa Rhine, wife of John B. Rhine, evaluated several thousand cases of spontaneous psi events and found that over half of them occurred during dreams. Most of these psi dreams were precognitive; they alerted the dreamer to events that later came true. These psi dreams varied in content. Some showed catastrophic incidents while others concerned minor, even trivial, situations. The individuals represented in these dreams were loved ones, acquaintances, or strangers.

Critics usually claim that people misinterpret coincidence as a psi event, but many of Louisa Rhine's cases involved highly unique incidents that were difficult to attribute to chance alone. Laboratory findings that support psi's existence argue in favor of such experiences being valid psi events.

In the 1960s, the Maimonides Medical Center in New York City formally tested the psi nature of dreams. Volunteers, who usually had no prior psi experience, spent the night in the laboratory, where the researchers used EEG instrumentation to study "dream telepathy." Whenever a REM cycle was observed, a researcher woke the subject and asked them to describe their dream. The objective of the experiment was to have the dreamer dream the target, usually an art print, that an assistant was observing in a distant room. A simple evaluation method was developed. The dreamer or an experimenter was employed to compare the dream material to four possible targets, one of which was the one used that night. The volunteer tried to identify the correct one. Guessing would result in one correct match for every four experiments, due to chance. An analysis of all their approximately three hundred experiments over ten years showed that one-third were successful, which is a significant deviation from chance. This overall result demonstrated that something beyond chance had occurred and that volunteers had often accessed the intended target while dreaming, though not every time.

While statistics made a case for psi occurring during dreams, examination of the actual dreams was even more convincing. In many cases, exact elements of the target were manifest in the dream action. Unusual, out-of-context dream elements proved to be the best clues for selecting the correct target. For example, a lion suddenly appears in a dream where the dreamer is walking with friends and talking about a baseball game they plan to attend. The lion is out of context. If the dreamer had no strong association to lions, then it is very likely the psi target is a scene with a lion or animals that resemble a lion.

Other dream researchers achieved both similar and contradictory results. Assuming appropriate experimental procedure was observed, this difference may have been due to a variety of reasons such as experimenter style, volunteer psi talent or motivation, type of target material, and the dreamer's environment. It is reasonable to expect that people can more easily experience psi dreams in the comfort of their own home than in a laboratory setting.

Most people who recall dreams having a psi element are struck by the dream's vividness, or at wake-up have strong intuitive feelings that alert them to the dream's psi nature. Many times, psi dreams are in direct response to a critical issue or concern, such as the well-being of a loved one who is far away.

Over the past half-century, progress has been made in understanding dreams and their practical use. Many dream workshops and dream programs exist that help people explore for themselves the many dimensions of dreams. As people work with dreams, they usually discover the dreams' psi potential. With a desire to explore psi dreaming, there is no reason why anyone, regardless of age or background, can't have psi enter in their dream state.

We all can discover the psi nature of our dreaming mind. Psi dreams can help us live more efficiently. They can even be lifesaving.

7

The Magician

HAROLD SHERMAN'S DREAM OF A NEAR-TRAGIC INCIDENT ON THE COPPERMINE RIVER indicated to me that dream content could be of psi origin. Louisa Rhine's research with spontaneous precognitive experiences as well as many other accounts of the psychic side of dreams showed that psi dreams often gave information of great value. They alerted the individual to approaching pleasant or unpleasant situations. In two-thirds of the cases where the individual acted on precognitive information, an accident or other unpleasant incident was avoided. Although I personally experienced psi-like dreams, they were unpredictable and difficult to identify as having their roots in psi. Nonetheless, I was convinced that psi dreams could occur more frequently if we consciously *chose* to have them.

When I began teaching "The Psychic Realm" course a few months after the Coppermine River journey, it became clear that a few people could consistently describe the key features of the intended target for the experiments I had set up. One class member in particular, Alison, did well when she was only slightly relaxed and when she was dreaming. After one class, Alison approached me with a challenge.

"Look," she said, "you have us doing our thing with your hidden targets. We're curious about you. Can you do what you so confidently are asking us to do? Can you take your own medicine? Do you know what doing psychic things feels like? Why don't *you* work on a psi target...one that we select?"

Her challenge surprised me. I still harbored resistance concerning my own psi, and about doing psi myself. I could see her point, but why look foolish (*that* again!) in front of the class? I was sure word would get out on how poorly—or well—I had done. So, even though Alison's request put me in a bind, why not?

I agreed, making it clear, however, that I was only exploring and did not care if I did well or not. It would be "for fun." I told her I was preoccupied with my work and community projects but thought I could work in an experiment or two.

"Remember what you tell us," she said, smiling. "The target can be anything."

The following evening I planned two approaches: I would seek impressions of her target both during a relaxed period and also while dreaming. At the agreed upon time, I retreated to my basement study and focused on seeing Alison's target, five miles away. I tried to relax, but had great difficulty. Too many thoughts rumbled through my mind—work issues, unfinished projects, and many other concerns. After forty-five minutes, I reached some degree of calmness, and a few faint images appeared, vague shapes that reminded me of elliptical eyeglasses, but not much more. Upon going to bed, I concentrated for several minutes on a desire to experience Alison's target in a dream and then fell asleep.

I awoke early in the morning, recalling no dream. It would be embarrassing to draw a blank, especially after my pep talk to the class. Disappointed, I drifted back to sleep. Shortly before the alarm rang, I woke up knowing I had had a lengthy, dramatic dream. But what had it been? I struggled to recall and in several minutes the dream came back to me in a flash:

I meet friends at a Holiday Inn to discuss psi topics. We enter the kitchen and order something. Across the courtyard I notice another dining area with vivid neon lights spelling out something that resembles the word Vic's. We walk into the lounge-dining room, which is full except for our table and the one next to it. A woman who resembles Alison sits down at that neighboring table and waves to get my attention. To my surprise, she ignores my return hand wave. I am disappointed.

She moves away. An amateur magician, who is now at that table, stands up and begins performing a magic act.

I watch him closely. Suddenly, to my surprise, he

strikes his forehead with the palms of his hands, then abruptly drops his arms. A messy, yellow, gel-like substance is smeared all over his forehead and it slowly drains across his face. Moving his lips, the magician begins to eat the gooey mess. Then he waves his arms and hands around dramatically, forms a cup shape with his palms, and ex-tends them directly toward me. A brilliant white spotlight flashes on and illuminates his cupped hands. I gaze into them, clearly seeing a large, white egg slowly growing out of his palms! I watch in amazement as the egg expands and becomes very large. He thrusts this egg close to my face and, with something like x-ray vision, I clearly see other eggs within the large one. He then sits down as the audience applauds loudly.

As soon as I had fixed the dream in memory, I jotted notes on my bedside pad. I recorded it in detail as soon as I could, later that morning. That evening, I reviewed my strange dream. At first it seemed too complex to match to any reasonable target. The more I examined it, however, the more I sensed themes and attention-calling action. The dream seemed to have elements symbolic of psi communication: friends who want to talk about psi topics; the woman who waves and then avoids normal communication; the magician and his feat; my x-ray vision.

Even though the dream was complex, it did emphasize one feature: eggs. The magician's complete, intense focus was on eggs that mysteriously appeared and multiplied; the yellow material running down his face, which he ate; the kitchen and dining room settings; and the sign—*Vic's*—associated to food of some type. Maybe her target was an elaborate restaurant scene. Maybe its central feature had egglike shapes or designs. Maybe I was totally wrong.

Was the dream about some aspect of myself? Perhaps I harbored a secret wish to be a stage actor? The dream was highly focused, unlike any other dream I could recall. If it was about Alison's target, what could it have been?

With great trepidation, I underlined the magician's "large, white egg," which didn't leave much room for error.

Later that night, I called Alison to learn ground truth...or maybe, instead, the bitter truth. I anxiously read my dream scenario to her.

Silence.

I finally spoke. "I don't know what your target was, or what you did, but the dream has all types of psi hints. I think the magician was dramatically trying to tell me something. Maybe your target was simple—was it a white egg, or eggs?"

Her response was sudden.

"I can't believe this!" she exclaimed. "You got the *exact target!* Shortly before our experiment began, I went to the refrigerator and brought out a carton of eggs...one dozen white eggs. I put them into a bowl, then I picked up two of them and squeezed them in my hands. I walked around the kitchen, tightly holding those eggs, visualizing you seeing them. I even imagined waving them in front of you, thrusting them toward your face."

I was stunned, speechless.

"Then, guess what...I couldn't resist," she continued. "I remembered you telling us about the emotional pick-up Harold Sherman had of you during your river journey, so I decided to add a bit of emotion to my unemotional eggs. I vividly imagined engaging you in an..."

"Don't say it, Alison," I shouted. "I know what you did. You envisioned hitting me with eggs—right on my forehead!"

"Yes. *Yes!* I pictured you sitting here in front of me. I visualized throwing eggs at your head. I even imagined smashing an egg on your forehead. I had a good old-fashioned egg battle...and you lost!"

I could easily imagine her doing this.

"I'll bet you thoroughly enjoyed that," I kidded her. "Now I can explain that yellow material running down the magician's face. It was egg yolk."

"Be glad it was only *dream* egg yolk," she said emphatically, "and that it ran over the magician's face, not yours!"

Both Alison and I were surprised at my egg dream. Even the faintly glimpsed pair of ovoid images that came to me during my relaxation period made sense.

Although a simple target, it made a clear point. Psi dreams occur when we have the *intention* to be open to them. They can be very accurate. You do not have to be a professional psychic to have them. Psi dreams can show us distant scenes that are unknown to us; they can present actions, emotions, and intentions of others. Sometimes they manifest complex dramatizations to emphasize a point. A psi symbol in a dream scenario can make it easy to identify the dream as including psi information.

I thanked Alison for choosing a simple, easy-to-evaluate target. Her creative enthusiasm and, I suspect, her ability in visualization, generated inner dynamics that helped me experience my first successful psi dream. After the magician dream, I wondered what all my initial discomfort had been about and why I feared looking foolish.

Now I knew what it felt like. The doctor had taken his own medicine, which would make it much easier to work with remote viewing and other psi data and eventually to understand some of psi's underlying psychodynamics. This experiment showed me that remote viewing and dreaming can compliment one another. I suspected that our strong intent for achieving psi contact was the key to success.

Alison had motivated me to experience a psi dream. This paved the way for me to begin new psi explorations, to see what I could discover, to see how psi dreams could be of help for anyone.

8
Silver Shell

A FEW MONTHS AFTER THE MAGICIAN DREAM, I RETURNED TO SRI FOR PROJECT-review meetings. I decided to remain aloof from direct involvement in any of their remote viewing experiments in order to avoid possible criticism of my objectivity. But I still recognized that my own inner exploration was vital for gaining insight into the psi process and giving me confidence with SRI's remote viewing research results. If others, including myself, could not duplicate their claims, then we would have a tough time challenging the critics' charge that SRI's results were not replicable. I hoped more people would be inspired to take a look at remote viewing, and that a multilaboratory approach would eventually provide confirmation of the SRI work.

How could I best explore psi directly? While I knew I could not take part in SRI's remote viewing projects, Alison's challenge had shown me a simple way to investigate psi—work with interested local people. Even on an informal basis, such activities could provide the insight I needed.

Even though I was overcoming my resistance to experiencing psi directly, I remained troubled. How does remote viewing—how does *psi*—work? The engineer-physicist in me continued to throw questions, perhaps doubts, in my path. I had tentative constructs: Perhaps a wavelike phenomenon similar to electromagnetics carries signals between minds? The mind may not be all "in the brain." We may all be part of a cosmic hologram. Something quantum physical, a "tunneling" effect similar to the way in which elementary particles move across boundaries, may have some role in psi phenomena.

My experience with the magician dream inclined me to consider something telepathic, possibly wavelike, at least for some aspects of psi. Although I may have sensed Alison's egg target through remote viewing, I had also sensed the invisible—her thoughts and intentions.

As I walked around Menlo Park those evenings, musing over possible mechanisms for explaining psi, an idea for a new experiment surfaced. This would make it possible to see what would happen with no sender or beacon person. Why not use a picture—one that hadn't been seen by any-one I knew—as a psi target? Someone could prepare a target picture and seal it in an unmarked, opaque envelope, without knowing what it was. That would be tricky, but it seemed feasible.

I was in the proper frame of mind for exploring psi and had spare time those evenings, so why not try an experiment on my own, totally indepen-dent of any formal activity at SRI?

The next day I asked an acquaintance to select a magazine he had not read and insert a bookmark at random into the magazine without looking at that page. There would be no way he could know the specific page and certainly not that page's content. Later that day he handed me a sealed package. Since he had not looked into the magazine, I couldn't access any information via his thoughts or knowledge.

This was just a trial experiment. If results were favorable, I would refine the procedure.

That evening I placed the envelope in a drawer in my motel room. My objective was to see if I could describe via psi any of the specific features on the designated page. If I could, telepathy from someone's mind could in no way account for the results. The target page had been randomly select-ed and had remained unobserved.

If my recorded impressions of the sealed target proved to be correct, then I had to consider the possibility of precognition as an explanation of the results. I may have been accessing my own future knowledge at the moment I opened and examined the target page. Some psi researchers suspect that precognition is fundamental to most types of psi experiences. It was difficult for me to imagine information coming toward me from the future, and I preferred to think that some type of real-time psi-scanning mechanism led to psi perception. However, this preference was probably due to my physics background, where cause-and-effect principles, even if unidentified, were assumed to exist for all phenomena. Psi scanning, though unexplainable, held promise for eventual discovery of its operating principle. Even if none could be found, psi scanning required relinquishing a hold on only one of the features of the universe—space. Bending the other feature of the universe—time—seemed to be much more improbable, at least to my somewhat conventional physics mentality. At that time, I thought precognition was contrary to free will, another troubling notion.

As I began to relax and seek impressions of the target, a rational thought intruded. What if the person who prepared the target had inadvertently caught a glimpse of the target page's edges? In that case, telepathy from him for some of the page's content could not be ruled out. To preclude this remote possibility, I decided to make the experiment extra hard. I focused on sensing only the key pictorial feature at, or very near, the exact center of the page. Of course, this presented a risk: Maybe the unknown page only had words, or there was no key feature on it at all. Nevertheless, I decided to go for the center.

Another potential problem presented itself: Perhaps I could detect something in the magazine, but on another page. A magazine usually has a hundred or more pages, and they are tightly stacked. How could I expect to sense the target page, when all that "noise" surrounded it? Even if I accessed the marked area, which of the two possible pages would it be? I decided the one on the right side as I opened the magazine would be the target.

As I tried to relax, my rational mind intruded again and I drifted into self-ridicule. This had to be the most absurd thing I'd ever tried to do. There was no way this experiment could work. There was no sender, no beacon person, and all those pages.

After that wave of doubt passed, I still could not relax. Eventually I went to bed, hoping I could experience a dream about the central feature on that target page. I focused on this objective frequently, and eventually drifted into a deep sleep. Late that night, I woke up with a start, or so it seemed. What first felt like being awake was actually a vivid dream. Gradually, I became aware I was "in a dream." I was having a lucid dream—that is, I knew I was dreaming—and I tried not to analyze the experience. In the past, too much thinking in a lucid dream brought it to a sudden end.

I am standing in a dimly lit room. It is empty except for a
small, square table directly ahead. Curious, I move toward
that table and note an object in the center. Suddenly, the
object becomes vivid and clear, as if illuminated by a
bright spotlight. I now see the object is in the shape of a
sea shell. It is silver-white.

On impulse, I slam my hand on the edge of the sea
shell. It flips up, turning over and over. I watch it fall
back toward the table's center and hear a loud clang when
it strikes. I watch, surprised, as the silver sea shell
wobbles awhile, and then becomes still. I hear someone say
it was a silver spoon. I reply, saying that it could be
better used as a large ashtray or a plate.

When I suddenly became aware I was in bed, I had no trouble recalling
that dream. I quickly turned on the light and sketched the silver sea shell I
had just seen. The vivid experience was energizing and I had trouble
returning to sleep. Once I did, however, I had a few more dreams, but they
were of routine situations.

I rose early that morning and wrote a detailed account of all my
dreams. I routinely keep track of remembered dreams, regardless of how
trivial they seem. At breakfast, I read and reread my dream journal. The
dream with the silver shell was unlike the others that were about routine
concerns. I suspected it might relate to the psi target.

The silver shell I had sketched resembled the scallop shell used by the
Shell gas company as its corporate logo. The vividness of the silver shell in
the lucid dream, and the reference to a silver spoon and large ashtray or
plate, made me suspect the dream image represented a plate or a dish,
not a sea shell. The dream's dramatic action—my striking the shell and
hearing its metallic sound—suggested it was made of metal, not ceramic
or glass. The dream's focus of a shell in the center of a square table hinted
of my dream intent: to detect only the key feature at the target page's
center.

As I reviewed my dream, I felt confident that something like a shell shape was at, or near, the center of the page. This left me no wiggle room. I was either completely wrong or right on. No shades of grey were possible. While I might quibble over interpretations, there could be not doubt about the sketch—I had drawn a sea shell, nothing else.

Maybe I had sensed the wrong page. I had decided in advance to look only at the marked page, not any other page in the magazine. If I sensed the wrong page, I would never know. Maybe this "no sender, no beacon person" approach to psi experiments was pure folly.

I returned from breakfast in a high state of angst. There was no way I could rationalize that dream. If it had no resemblance to the target page, what *was* it about? Something symbolic about my inner state? There was more on the line than I had anticipated. I had to experience psi directly in order to maintain motivation in my official remote viewing project work. I needed help bolstering my sometimes shaky confidence against the vigorous thrust of the ever-ready critics. Even if it was not perfect match, I could only hope that shell correlated with something on that page.

I retrieved the sealed package, carefully opened it, and pulled out the magazine. The cover had been removed by my colleague so that he would not think about the cover picture or any feature article announcements. I gently placed the magazine on a small table. The moment of truth had arrived; I could not procrastinate any longer. I had to learn the truth, *now.* Quickly I opened it at the marker and stared at the right-side page.

What I saw was stunning! In the exact center of the picture, propped in the center of a wooden display case, was a beautiful silver sea shell! The entire page was an advertisement for Gorham pewter—knives, forks, spoons, and plates were in the display case and on a table in the foreground. My sketch of the shell was off by only one-eighth of an inch in its diameter. An odd marking I had drawn on the shell corresponded to an overlap by another item. The dream act of striking the shell carried two messages: First, it had shown me that the object was metal, and second, it was a sign that I had "hit" the target.

This experiment had a powerful effect on me. I could now sense the vastness of the psi domain. At least for some psi experiences, I had to suspend simple notions of a sender or beacon person. Alison's visualization of throwing eggs in the magician dream made a strong case for the role of a sender. My silver-shell dream, however, had no apparent sender and fit the concept of remote viewing. Now I had to maintain an openness to two modes of psi-seeing: (1) something like telepathy; and (2) something like clairvoyance or remote viewing. If my dream experience was precognitive, it could have been derived from my future knowledge—something like telepathy from the future. Reluctantly, I began to consider precognition as another possible psi process.

The silver shell dream opened up new avenues for my personal psi exploration. I could now work independent of others. It would be easy to set up tightly controlled experiments using sealed pictures and work on them at a convenient, leisurely pace. Picture-target pools could be developed easily. Pictures as psi targets simplified data evaluation. The target is clearly defined on a single page. Picture targets reduce logistics and cost, since travel to a real site for feedback is not necessary. A picture can be mailed or faxed for feedback. For real-site remote viewing projects, data evaluation could be difficult. A target area is often complex with features that resemble aspects of other sites used in a target pool.

Both picture targets and real-world sites are important for understanding psi. Picture-target pools could be constructed to give insight on cognitive preferences and on phenomenon variables or limitations. Real-world targets give insight into practical-application issues since most potential applications probably involve complex areas and unexpected situations.

In the years ahead, I refined procedures in order to assure that sensory leakage was not the underlying reason for success. I worked on hundreds of psi experiments. Some targets were thousands of miles away. Some had observers; others were unknown, sealed in envelopes. A few targets were in difficult locations, like secure vaults or deep in the ocean.

The Magician and Silver Shell dreams were milestone experiences in my psi exploration. I felt then, and still do, like a tracker squinting toward faint prints—a tracker who keeps returning for a better look, a better understanding of what has passed by, and what might be ahead.

9

Trouble in
Reactor Bay

ED MITCHELL'S EXPERIMENT FROM SPACE DURING THE APOLLO 14 MISSION AND
Sir Hubert Wilkins and Harold Sherman's Arctic experiment inspired me to
explore the communication potential of psi. My Arctic search adventure
with Harold in 1976 gave me insight into psi's potential for search and rescue. The remote viewing research at SRI continued to produce data showing potential for narrowing search options had it been applied to search-
and-rescue missions.

I could see the possibility for applying remote viewing to Air Force
operational needs. Occasionally airplanes are lost. Some people suspect
that pilots are still held in Southeast Asia. I anticipated returning to the
Arctic, and like Sir Hubert had done, wanted to keep an option open for psi
contact should we become lost. Frequently volunteer search-and-rescue
teams were called into mountainous areas to look for missing hikers or
children that wandered away. I could easily envision a variety of practical,
worthwhile applications for remote viewing phenomena.

The psi data I had examined suggested a one-way type of contact or
communication had occurred with the distant site or individuals at that site.
I wondered if it was possible to pursue search-and-rescue or other psi
tasks on a two-way basis? Maybe both the searchers and those wanting to
be found could participate in the psi process. If it is possible for the lost
persons to unknowingly be involved at a subconscious level, why couldn't
this also happen at a conscious level?

In addition to whatever psi mechanism was involved for accessing a
distant scene, why not have remote viewers seek specific messages of

the intent or status of those at the unknown place? Why not have those missing, via their own psi, seek information about the search situation, or sense and receive messages from the psi search team?

My Silver Shell experience demonstrated that a sender was not necessary, but this led to a conceptual difficulty: Since remote viewing research showed that a beacon person was not necessary, then how can a message from someone's intention be sensed by a remote viewer? Furthermore, research also showed that literal messages—sentences or numbers, for example—are very difficult to detect reliably. Forms and shapes work well, but not logical sequences of information. Even so, my informal exploratory work with students in "The Psychic Realm" course showed that message sending was possible and the magician dream carried a clear message of Alison's intent and her envisioned activity.

Psi data suggested that at least two modes or principles could be operative: (1) impersonal remote viewing of the environment, which did not seem to depend on anyone's knowledge, and (2) personal, mindlike contact for intentions or feelings. Why not assume both principles can be operative and give both mindlike and environment, or spacelike, data the opportunity to reveal themselves? Useful information could originate from a beacon person's knowledge or from the site. Maybe these apparent differences only reflect personality and preferences in cognitive style.

The idea of mindlike and spacelike data appealed to my physics background. Light has two aspects: particle and wave. In quantum physics, the position (spacelike) and momentum (motion) of a particle are different attributes of that particle that cannot be accurately known simultaneously. Before measurement can be accomplished, a decision must be made which of the two are to be sought. Could a psi-wave exist that, similar to light, carries form or spacelike and motionlike information (emotions and feelings)? Maybe only one can be sensed at any instant, but not the other. Some people with psi talent might naturally resonate with one type while others might do well with both.

After Arctic Search, I developed plans for a two-way psi-communication experiment for either remote viewing or dreaming. The objective of this project was to explore the potential of psi for relaying messages between distant locations. Since words and sentences are unreliable for psi perception, pictures or real sites would have to be used as primary psi targets. A printed message would then be associated with that picture or site. Should the remote viewer or dreamer perceive the target accurately, the message from the person at the distant location could be determined by checking a duplicate list of target-message possibilities. This list would be available to the remote viewer or dreamer or to someone else at the message-receiving location. With remote viewers or dreamers at both locations, this technique could be used for message exchange.

For example, someone one thousand miles away from a remote viewer looks at a picture of the Statue of Liberty that has the desired message printed on its reverse side. If the remote viewer perceives "something like a tall statue" and chooses the Statue of Liberty picture from among the other possibilities in the picture-message pool, then he or she flips it over and reads the intended message. Thus, a message such as "I am lost in a mountain area," would be relayed.

To make this message-relay technique feasible, the target pool and preselected message possibilities would have to be limited to only a few. This would increase the chance of selecting the message picture correctly. A large set of targets with overlapping features would be difficult to narrow down. For a series of messages, it would be necessary to set time windows for message sending or exchange in advance.

I had often envisioned applying such a message technique to communicating with isolated people, such as hostages or prisoners of war. It seems to me that their involvement in such an activity could help them maintain hope, even if rescue action could not be taken immediately. Individuals traveling to high-risk areas could be trained in sending, or focusing on sending, messages to a psi search team.

Earlier, I had come across Soviet research on thought transmission of objects, which showed psi-communication potential. Some Soviet psi researchers had shown interest in applying this simple technique for communication with spacecraft and submarines but no data was available on how specific messages would be exchanged. I began to wonder if my envisioned psi-communication experiment could be set up between remote military sites or between ships or submarines and shore locations.

In a few weeks, I received a call from Hal Puthoff informing me that an unexpected opportunity had come up. He had a chance to schedule a remote viewing experiment on a deep-ocean research submersible that had the capability of diving thousands of feet below sea level. The submersible's primary task was deep-ocean archaeological exploration in one thousand feet of water near Catalina Island, California, five hundred miles from the SRI laboratory. The opportunity was offered by Stephan Schwartz, an independent investigator and entrepreneur who had chartered the vessel.

I wholeheartedly supported this venture. Two of SRI's remote viewers would be on board the submersible over a weekend that July. While on board, their primary task was remote viewing of the ocean floor to help locate sunken artifacts. A secondary objective was remote viewing of natural targets in the San Francisco Bay area. If the remote viewing experiments succeeded, the phenomenon was very likely not electromagnetic, since most electromagnetic frequencies would be attenuated and blocked at one thousand feet below sea level, in salt water.

Hal's call gave new life to my dream for demonstrating psi's communication potential. I quickly developed procedures for a two way–communication experiment, both from shore to submersible and submersible to shore. The two-way message-sending technique would be incorporated into the remote viewing protocol as a third goal only if it would not interfere with anything else. Shore-to-submersible message sending would be based on natural scenes in the San Francisco Bay area. The submersible-to-shore message plan had to be based on pictures on-board the submersible.

I traveled out to SRI to help coordinate and to observe the weekend experiment directly. Hella Hammid and Ingo Swann were the remote viewers on board the submersible.

The first remote viewing target site was a giant oak tree on a hilltop in Potola Valley. At the same time the beacon person was at that site, Hella described "a very tall, looming object. A very, very huge tree and a lot of space behind it." The message corresponding to that site was "Remain at sea three more days."

The second remote viewing target was the interior of a well-designed shopping mall in Mountain View, California. While on the submersible, Ingo described and sketched "flat, stone flooring, walls, small pool, reddish stone walk, large doors, walking around an enclosed space." The message corresponding to that site was "Proceed to Rendezvous X."

When the remote viewers were shown pictures of the six target possibilities, they had no difficulty selecting the correct ones. This indicated that, had a real message from shore been intended, the remote viewers could have determined what it was even though they were five hundred miles away and submerged under one thousand feet of ocean water.

Later, when I saw their sketches, I also had no trouble choosing the correct site. I had purposely kept myself blind to the actual targets so that I could be an evaluator.

This portion of the experiment showed that sending messages to submarines or space vehicles via psi was possible as a simple back-up to conventional means. All that would be needed on-board was a remote viewer and a set of well-constructed pictures or scenes that corresponded with specific messages.

The plan for submersible-to-shore message sending was simple also, requiring only a separate picture-message codebook for the remote viewer or dreamer on shore. Anyone on board could select a message from the options available and pull that message envelope from the file of possibilities. He or she could either look at the corresponding picture or keep it in its sealed envelope. The task for a remote viewer or dreamer on shore would be to describe or sketch that on-board picture target at an agreed-upon time. If the sketch matched any of those in an identical message codebook on shore, then the message associated with that picture could be read. That message would relate to the status of the submarine at that time and it could be a lengthy description or a simple statement.

There was interest in my submersible-to-shore message project, but no remote viewer was available at the SRI laboratory. In the event we found a remote viewer in time, one of the experimenters who would be aboard the submersible had prepared a set of six sealed pictures. When the on-board team departed for Los Angeles and the submersible, we still did not have a viewer at the SRI laboratory.

This presented a major dilemma. As contract manager, I did not want to be involved as a remote viewer. I knew the U.S. Navy was too political and image sensitive to consider such an experiment. This opportunity could be the only one in the foreseeable future—how could I pass it up? However, I had no track record in remote viewing. Those few experiments I had done did not seem to be sufficient for me to be chosen as the submersible-to-shore message seeker. With great trepidation and all kinds of qualifiers, I agreed to give it a try nonetheless. Pleased with my decision, Hal contacted Dr. Edwin May, the on-board experimenter, before he left port to tell him the submersible-to-shore message-sending experiment was a go.

Three messages would be selected during the craft's submersion: one on Saturday afternoon, one Sunday morning, and the last on Sunday afternoon. I would have three chances to do my thing. The crew would return by Tuesday, when we would all learn ground truth.

Since I had plenty of time, I planned on two approaches for sensing the on-board message picture. The first was to relax, remote viewing style, and hope to receive relevant impressions. The other was to perceive the targets in dreams. I was interested in comparing data from these two ways of perceiving psi data.

Dr. May decided not to open the target envelope for my task. He was concerned that the picture might somehow interfere with the on-board remote viewers during their attempts to describe the on-shore target sites. Thus, no one on board would be observing the target. Had it not been for the Silver Shell dream experience, I would have had little confidence in this no-sender approach.

Saturday morning I walked around to squelch a growing tension. I tried a strategy that eliminated the "butterflies" and helped me set focus on the objective. While walking, I occasionally concentrated on the goal, then relaxed and let my thoughts drift about randomly. I tried to maintain a light mood; after all, this was not a weighty situation—it was okay to fail...it was okay to succeed. I simply wanted to discover what could be done, to communicate with that submarine and to see their "message of the day."

Shortly after Saturday noon, I pulled the curtains tight and tried to relax in my darkened motel room. All I could do was hope...and wait. Should anything appear, I wanted it to be of the message target, not any of the countless trillions of other possibilities in the universe. To my surprise, I quickly relaxed. In just moments, a few faint impressions appeared: someone, a woman, was very seasick. I felt a surge of nausea, and was unable to remain relaxed. Some time later I felt fine and once again drifted into a relaxed state. Then impressions came: a dark-haired woman in white slacks; a well-decorated room; a long, cylindrical, shiny object; then several shiny objects that seemed to be falling. I heard a very loud banging or booming noise which distracted me, and I lost focus. Since there had been no loud noise outside my room, I suspected it was an "internal noise."

After an hour or so, I could no longer hold focus. I walked around for several hours, had a light dinner, and went to bed early, hoping the message picture would present itself in a dream. I slept well.

My first dream, late that night, was very dramatic:

I am in a modern house when it is suddenly destroyed. Glass shatters all around; a wall explodes outward; loud banging noises come from the ceiling and it collapses. I look up and see an open sky. Outside I see men wearing World War II uniforms.

My second dream occurred right before the alarm and was very peaceful:

I am in a well-lit room with three washbowls. Tall mirrors cover three of the walls. Someone is cleaning small rock-like objects in water running from a faucet.

Soon after recording these disturbing impressions, I had to get in the mood for the Sunday-morning experiment. As I was not at all sleepy, I knew I could not rely on the dream state. Relaxed images came almost immediately. They were clear and vivid: golden curls...a patterned handbag...the face of a pretty woman with long golden hair.

I took a break and sketched these impressions as accurately as I could, then went back to the task. In a few minutes, another clear image popped into view: a large, round, dark face, with thick, dark areas around the eyes and a very prominent, flat and wide nose. I broke relaxation and sketched these unusual animal-like features.

The first image was clearly that of a pretty, golden-haired woman. The second image looked exactly like a gorilla. I began to wonder about the devious mind that constructed the target pool. Maybe I should have been concerned about something in me instead.

A bit groggy from all that relaxing, I took a long walk. I had decided to forgo lunch. I was concerned that food might cause me to feel too lethargic during my third, and final, attempt for another message from the "submarine." My afternoon relaxing session was unproductive. I kept seeing, over and over, the earlier images of the golden-haired woman and could not get her out of my mind. I cut the session short, went for a long walk, had a light evening meal, and went to bed early. Thoughts of seeing the ship's message pictures filled my mind as I drifted to sleep. I only woke from one brief dream late that morning:

```
I am looking at a complex painting that I had just com-
pleted. Its broad, rectangular-shaped border is filled with
diagonal bands of black and white. The interior is a com-
plex pattern of multicolored strands of odd, bright-yellow
shapes with alternating black and white centers. I touch
it. It feels smooth, glossy, and thick. I begin to think it
is a smooth, linoleum-covered floor. With no warning, some-
one grabs the painting, rolls it up, and steps on it. When
it does not crackle or tear, I realize it is made of thick
fabric, not linoleum.
```

I was amazed at the vividness and complexity of this dream. After sketching it in great detail and annotating the color areas, I went to breakfast. I felt refreshed and had a sense that something might come of my wild idea for detecting messages from a submarine. At breakfast, over many cups of coffee, I refined my sketches of that dream painting. The more I considered it, the more I began to think the dream artwork was not a paint-ing, but a rug. The idea of linoleum, later corrected by someone rolling it and stepping on it, hinted of a rug, not a painting.

I could hardly wait for the submersible's crew to return. Much too soon, Hal called me into the room with the six target pictures arranged randomly on a table. The person who removed them from their envelopes had the key identifying the three correct targets, which even Hal did not know.

As we talked, I recalled that wave of nausea and the image of a woman who was very seasick when I began the experiment. I learned that Hella had become very seasick and had almost cut her participation short.

I sat at the table and gazed around. So there they were, all six of the possibilities. Based on my images and dreams, could I find the right three and thereby know what those three "desperate" messages were from that "lost" submarine crew? I resisted making a selection at first. Did I want to know the truth or not?

I looked at my first dream impressions of destruction and shattering glass and the second dream impressions of a modern glass or mirror-filled kitchen. I was not sure that the relaxation imagery of a dark-haired woman in a well-decorated room, and a long, shiny cylinder related to the dreams. One picture showed several large, glass bottles, which I chose. My second choice was a picture of a B-1 and a B-52 aircraft, which resembled the images of the long, shiny cylinder and reminded me of bombing missions and destruction. The B-52 in the picture was dropping bombs, but no destruction was visible.

I looked at my sketches of the golden-haired woman and the gorilla. There was only one possibility—a picture of a blonde woman holding a pat-terned handbag standing next to a gorilla! Needless to say, that was my choice. It had to be a direct hit.

I had trouble finding a clear match for the third message, which came as a surprise since the dream of the thick fabric had been so vivid. The only possibility I saw was a picture of a volleyball court with a thick net and a player. Due to the net's configuration dominance, I chose that, but I did not feel confident. There was no clear second choice.

I listed only my first and second choices. However, in a real situation, you either get the correct message or you don't. Anxiously I waited for ground truth. An assistant, who did not know my selections, entered the room. He gave me a sealed envelope with a duplicate list of the correct pictures and their corresponding messages. I gave him a list of my selections. Then I opened the envelope and received ground truth.

My selection for the Saturday afternoon message had been a miss. The correct message picture was my second choice, the B-52. I was extremely disappointed. I looked at the key for Saturday night's picture. The blonde woman and the gorilla was the correct target picture. I read the corresponding message:

We Are Back on Track: Moving to Deep Rift Checkpoint.

Getting two out of three messages would make my day. Anxiously, I checked the list. My first choice was the correct one! Referring to the picture-message key, I read the message sent from deep in the ocean:

Trouble in Reactor Bay: Condition Serious Red.

A tremendous pressure wave suddenly released its hold from my mind and body. This wild idea *did* work! The images, especially of the golden-haired woman and gorilla, pushed the experiment way beyond good guessing. What was the probability of those images occurring now? So far, people or animals had not been included in the laboratory target pool. I would not have guessed such a picture would be in that target set.

I called Hal into the room and showed him the results. This was truly a great moment, yet I knew something as significant as communication to or from a submarine could not be demonstrated by one brief experiment with just a few trials. Hal left the room to attend to other business, but I remained awhile, simply staring at the pictures and their associated messages. Casually I picked up the target pictures for a closer look and made a surprising discovery.

Other vivid pictures were on the reverse sides. These targets had remained unopened while on board the submersible. The on-board experimenter said that he systematically displayed the front side of the envelope but did he? When he opened the envelopes on shore, did he keep the proper side up? How was I to know which target was "up"? Maybe there had been twelve possible target pictures, not just six.

With renewed interest, I took a close look at the B-52 target picture, then turned it over. On the reverse was a brightly lit kitchen with large stove panels. A dark-haired woman in a white outfit is holding a plate of vegetables. The ceiling is not visible.

I was stunned. I must have sensed both sides of the target page and my first dream combined my impressions of both of them. My association to the B-1 and B-52 as bombers, and memories of movies showing World War II bombing missions, influenced the dream dynamics and led to a scene of destruction. In the picture, the B-52 was shown dropping bombs. I now understood what those presleep viewing images represented. The long, cylindrical, shiny object resembled the airplane fuselage and the bombs. However, I had not perceived them clearly enough to identify them as an airplane or a bomb.

The second dream—a peaceful kitchen with washbowls, mirrors, and someone cleaning small rocklike objects under a faucet—kept the focus on only one side of the target page. Had I looked at the opposite side initially, I would have had another direct hit. I know I would have selected that picture as the target.

The opposite side of the picture of the blonde-haired woman and gorilla had no competing imagery, only words and blank areas. That made it easy. But the opposite side of the rectangular floor or painting held another shock: It was a full-page view of a beautiful blanket with a Native American–style pattern that matched very closely the complex shapes I had drawn and the colors I had seen in the dream. Shapes and forms from both sides of the page seemed to have entered into my impressions. The two similar forms—rectangular painted floor and the rectangular blanket—may have enhanced the psi signal and led to that vivid dream. This experiment taught us a valuable lesson: Be sure the intended target pictures have no competing elements on the reverse side!

Even though I only chose two of the three targets, it was very clear that I would have had three direct hits had I initially looked at both sides. My experimental emergency-communication scenario had succeeded. In this scenario, an anxious crew in deep water sent out their frantic message to an intensely interested, receptive, person thousands of miles away. Safely on shore, he is the only person to know the truth about the disappearance of that submarine. Twenty years after demonstrating this simple submarine-to-shore backup communication technique, that individual still hears echoes of that crew's final plight:

```
Trouble in Reactor Bay: Condition Serious Red.
```

Our psi communication experiment with this submersible showed the potential for real applications. Using psi techniques, specific messages could be relayed between remote locations, including deep-ocean vessels. Proper picture-message selection could be used to learn the status from, or provide instructions to, that distant place. With proficiency, and a larger set of picture-message possibilities, information for locating individuals in difficult areas, such as a jungle or broad ocean areas, could be possible.

In my visions, I see groups of people openly exploring two-way psi communication. A team committed to that objective, free of biases, and openly exploring, is achieving the direct exchange of reliable messages, both pictures and words, between distant locations. The potential for two-way psi communication has been accepted by a variety of individuals—pilots flying over remote areas, submarine crews, explorers, travelers, or others in areas where hostage taking could occur. With a core group of psi sensitives and a common set of picture-message possibilities unique to each situation, they are prepared to use psi communication in emergencies.

In my visions, I also see a hostage focusing on an appropriate picture message to provide health status:

```
I am in good condition.
```

His next message gives his general location:

```
I am near a large river.
```

A series of messages provides enough information for search-and-rescue action and lead to his return. Similarly, the captive, who is trained in psi techniques, perceives picture messages held by someone on the search team and determines the search status:

```
Rescue attempt pending.
```

Ed Mitchell's intuitive sense for using psi to communicate with distant spacecraft, and Harold Sherman and Sir Hubert Wilkins's dream of establishing psi communication between remote regions on Earth, have become a reality. Their work, along with other human-potential achievements, have become recognized as benchmarks for charting our role in the evolution of consciousness. Their tracks and those of other pioneers are more readily seen, accepted, and followed.

10
Tall Black Figure

A FEW WEEKS AFTER SILVER SHELL, I WAS IN LOS ANGELES ON A TECHNOLOGY business trip. Discussions of technical issues, presentations, and evening social activities with colleagues filled the week. I had planned to return to Dayton on Saturday, and looked forward to a free Friday evening to unwind from the busy schedule.

I looked forward to that Friday night for another reason. Before leaving Dayton, I had arranged a psi experiment with Alison. She planned to describe my activities one midweek evening and I was to try to describe a target she would choose that Friday. I was sure I could not get into a mood that would be appropriate for working with psi any earlier than Friday evening.

I asked Alison just to hold the target in mind and not to make a draw-ing, look at an object or picture, or perform any physical activity, as she had for the magician dream. I wanted to see if mental thoughts or images alone could be detected. The additional challenge of a three-thousand-mile distance would make this experiment especially interesting.

As chairman of the Radar and Optical Data Technical Group, during my stay in Los Angeles, I had little time for anything but business. As the week wore on, I looked forward to Friday evening and a break from the fast-paced activities. Even though I routinely recorded my activities and dreams in a journal, I recalled no dreams and ignored my daily writing that week—until Thursday night. By that time, I was exhausted. Returning late to the hotel, I looked forward to a good night's sleep and concluding the next day. I had no intention for dream recall.

I woke up shortly before the alarm rang, having been startled by a vivid and unusual dream.

I am in a classroom, ready to begin a presentation for my "Psychic Realm" course. The classroom is full. Someone expresses thanks for my lecture and my experiential approach. I hear a noise at the door, and glance around.

Startled, I watch the door slowly open. An incredibly tall black man enters. He is extremely thin and must be ten feet tall or more. The only way he can come into the room is by leaning forward. He walks toward me, stooping to avoid the ceiling. I stretch up on tiptoes to get a closer look. He is dressed in black clothes that resemble a clergyman's outfit and has very large, owl-like eyes. I am not afraid and I feel a deep sense of peace. He invokes a calming effect on me and the class.

As he leans over, he begins to whisper. I can hardly hear him. Faintly, I hear him give advice for someone he says is reaching people in deeper ways than most can. He continues: "Do not worry about others as long as your experiences are not seen as only yours."

Then, stooping low, he turns and walks out of the room.

I woke up amazed. The dream was different from all other dreams. I had no association to a very tall, black clergyman. The dream did not make sense, even from a symbolic point of view. I did not understand what was meant by the dream figure's words. All I could do was record the details and wait. Maybe time would provide clarification.

I frequently thought of the dream during that day and was puzzled by it. I had planned to relax on my own, that evening, but social obligations won out. I did not return to the hotel until after midnight. An evening of too much food and wine stifled any strong desire to try Alison's experiment. Even though I made a feeble attempt to perceive psi impressions of Alison's target, I overslept and had to dash to catch the morning flight to Dayton. Reluctantly, I had to take a pass on what I had hoped would be a very interesting transcontinental psi experiment.

Early the following week, I called Alison to see if she had sensed any aspects of my Wednesday-evening activities in Los Angeles. The week had not been a good one for her. Several unexpected demands and a minor illness kept her from trying the experiment. I explained that I, too, was distracted and unable to work on my part of the Friday night experiment with her target.

"By the way," she said, shortly before we were to hang up, "I should tell you something. When I learned I would be on a trip over the weekend, starting Friday, I suspected I would be unable to focus on our experiment on Friday night, so I selected a target for you on Thursday, and hoped you would still be able to get it on Friday."

Something was beginning to make sense. I listened anxiously as she continued.

You said you did not even try on Friday, so I guess my intention did not come through," she said, wistfully.

Memories were returning.

"Guess what, Alison, although I had no impressions on Friday, I had a most unusual dream experience on Thursday. I can't imagine it could have anything to do with your intended target."

"Was it really strange?" she quizzed.

"That it was," I said.

Her response was quick. "Well, then, I suspect you got the target!" she exclaimed.

"Alison, was your target about a very tall person?"

"Yes! Yes! You got it!" she shouted.

"On Thursday evening, I decided to choose a person as a target. So far we have been working with objects or scenes. I wanted this to be so unique that no one, not even you, could have any doubts. That evening, I relaxed and mentally reviewed the target I intended you to see. I imagined it over and over, for about fifteen minutes. The target I wanted you to see was an imaginary being—a very tall, black man with very large eyes.

"I had no picture or drawing. I simply created a mental image of a tall, stick-thin, black man dressed in a priest's outfit. I imagined seeing you in your motel room and having the tall figure lean over and walk toward you."

Quietly, I listened on in disbelief.

"I imagined him bending close to your face."

I could not believe what she was saying. "Don't tell me, Alison, that you had your tall black figure talk to me," I said, incredulously.

"Yes! I imagined him giving you an answer to some questions I have. One had to do with a friend of mine. Another had to do with a concern of mine."

Regaining my composure, I related the brief personal message I heard in the dream about someone reaching people in deeper ways than most can. It seemed appropriate and offered insight into the situation faced by her friend, whom Alison had been helping with personal issues. It seemed that our minds had linked for this experiment and that the tall black figure she envisioned became a dream figure for conveying her subconscious knowledge.

"What was the other question?" I asked, cautiously.

She paused awhile, then slowly continued.

"You and I are from totally different backgrounds. Yours is physical science–based, mine is esoteric and metaphysical. Some of my metaphysical books make quite an issue 'of doing psychic things,' especially psychic experiments. So my other question was: Is it okay for me to continue doing psi experiments?"

I thought long and carefully about my response.

"Alison, let's start with what I heard in that dream. Clearly that was a psi dream; I sensed exactly what you intended. Maybe we did access something beyond our own surface egos and the dream figure's whisper is a good answer: 'Do not worry about others as long as your experiences are not seen as only yours.' I read that as saying it is okay as long as you and I share our psi explorations and use psi to help ourselves and others."

Those words made sense to both of us.

We talked for a long time, pondering the implications of our long-distance psi experiment. If Alison and I could establish a clear psi link, others certainly could do the same. We wondered why people generally were reluctant to explore their psi potential and suspected deep-seated resistances held them back.

Negative views of psi from influential people—some leading scientists, religious spokespeople, parents—could cause some of their concerns. Certain vocal critics stated that belief in psi was irrational and then used irrational arguments to attack psi. Psi phenomena can be considered as nonrational—that is, beyond rational explanation—but not as irrational. Sensationalistic media presentations, which use a fear perspective, contribute to the general disregard of psi potential. The best course of action, it seemed to us, was to ignore biases against psi and simply take a look; explore psi to see what is true or false.

Alison's concern about doing psi experiments came from viewpoints she encountered in some of the historic metaphysical literature she had studied. This material cautioned against seeking psi experiences, since they were seen to distract the individual from transcendental pursuits. Certainly a balanced approach to the pursuit of psi was necessary.

Some esoteric practitioners were especially negative toward psi experiments. They felt that psi was a special gift that should not be used for psi experiments, which they considered trivial. I suspected that some of these individuals did not want to attempt psi experiments only to discover that their data was not as accurate as they claimed...or hoped.

I explained to Alison that psi events occurred to many people spontaneously, for both significant and minor situations. Aboriginal cultures still relied on their psi talents for food gathering or survival in general. We agreed that psi phenomena had to be a fundamental aspect of the universe that could be used for practical purposes, even if its occurrence is usually hidden. The universe did not seem to be constructed with useless phenomena.

It is impossible to know what the future will bring regarding the possible integration of physical and metaphysical views. Quantum physicists may be supplementing the role of early philosophers. What is the nature of the universe? Is the cosmos an intricate web of pulsating energies, as some metaphysicians have suspected?

Thus far in our experiments, we discovered that by going inward to explore psi we had touched deep roots at personal and transpersonal levels. This seemed to be one of the main goals of metaphysical pursuits.

Alison and I talked about the role of research in the discovery of fundamental truths about the nature of reality. Quantum physics included concepts that seemed more metaphysical than real. The subatomic world that physics describes seems ghostly, filled with shadowy things that flit quickly between existence and nonexistence. Great advances such as the laser and computer technology have resulted from research into quantum physics. This new understanding came from an experimental approach that began by examining anomalies—phenomena that did not fit into conventional understanding of classical physics. We wondered what new understanding of the universe would evolve from an experimental approach in examining psi phenomena. Perhaps the distinction between physical and metaphysical reality might become blurred, with new understanding of one supplementing the understanding of the other.

It seemed to us that psi was a natural part of the universe, more like a talent than a special gift. The consideration of psi as only a special gift carried implications of elitism that was contrary to the natural, democratic nature of other phenomena in the universe. We knew that psi often made its presence known through hunches and intuitions and occasionally through synchronicities and luck. Psi, as a natural but latent talent, could be uncovered by anyone with a balanced approach.

I ended our long discussion by returning to the question she had posed about doing psi experiments.

"Alison," I said, "as long as we develop a sense of connectivity or empathy with others and with our environment, and maintain a balanced lifestyle, we will want to help others and to share what we discover. Our psi sensitivities are an aid to, not a distraction from helping us live more effectively. The metaphysical concerns you raised may be a reminder to have a clear, positive purpose in psi activities, and to call attention to the need for balance and sharing."

"I see your point," she said, after a few moments. "With sharing and balance, or grounding, psi or any inner exploration activity, can be positive, can help us evolve."

This experiment turned out to be far more than the interesting long-distance psi exploration I originally intended. I gained insight into the power our thoughts and visualization can have, even when the people involved are separated by great distance. In addition, Allison could now deal with a concern shared by many people who begin psi exploration. We felt like explorers and wondered what new discoveries would eventually be found in the psi domain.

Psi phenomena may be the "glue that binds"—the interface between—the physical and the metaphysical. Maybe the key to future survival on this planet is the better understanding and the use of our intuitive and psi potential. Psi knows no boundaries, has no walls. As Robert Frost said in his poem "Mending Wall": "Something there is that doesn't love a wall, that wants it down." Psi is like a truth-seeking chisel that enters the cracks of the walls that we all try to build.

A balanced approach to psi, along with concern and caring for others, our environment, and our planet, can bring down those walls.

11
Not-So-Far Side

MY APPROACH TO DREAMWORK IS TO EXAMINE THE DREAM FROM TWO PERSPECTIVES: First, does it relate to personal issues and concerns? and second, does it have psi potential, including the precognitive form? When I suspect a dream to be of psi origin, I mark it as such in my dream journal and enter a summary on a separate list for quick reference. For precognitive dreams, timing presents a major problem as it is difficult to tell when a future event will occur. If the dream is of a warning nature, I will consider ways to avoid the dream situation. After a few weeks, if the dream does not correlate with an event I learn about or encounter, I review it from a personal point of view. It may have represented an aspect of myself or a relationship that I had not grasped.

Some precognitive dreams are literal and specific. They are easy to recognize. Others are incomplete or symbolic and may not be recognized as precognitive. We can puzzle over these and await possible developments, or we can intend to have a new dream that clarifies the puzzling one.

I look at precognitive dreams from three perspectives: (1) an already formed incident coming my way; (2) an incident that, with searching, could be found to have a contemporary cause somewhere; and (3) an incident that was essentially impossible to trace to any emerging situation anywhere.

A classic example of an already-formed precognitive dream is that of Lincoln's death dream ten days before his assassination. This dream had a profound impact on the president and was unlike any he had previously experienced, even during the height of the Civil War. In this dream, he heard subdued sobs, saw a body wrapped in funeral vestments in the East

Room, and heard a guard say: "the president is dead . . . killed by an assassin." Many writers consider this to be precognitive, but I see it as a contemporaneous psi experience. John Wilkes Booth had formed his intention prior to the night of Lincoln's dream. Nothing could alter his plan and Lincoln sensed his intention through telepathy.

Mark Twain's oft-quoted precognitive dreams of reading letters that he later received had contemporary links. Either a letter writer intended to pen it or had actually sent it in the mail at the time of Mark Twain's dream. While such dreams depict unknown future events for the dreamer, they are not unknown futures for the instigators. Mark Twain probably sensed the contents of the approaching letters by telepathy or remote viewing.

The second type of precognitive dream—an incident that requires searching to find an initiating circumstance somewhere—is difficult to reconcile in terms of telepathy or remote viewing. Even if root links can be found, we may have had an unconscious role in causing that experience. This could be interpreted as something like unconscious wish-fulfillment via psi. The resulting precognitive experience may be a valid psi event, but we may have had a role in its perpetration.

For example, you may have a dream of an acquaintance you have not seen in years. The next day you go into a restaurant you rarely visit and see that person. Very likely, your subconscious impulses led you to deviate from your routine at the right time to have that dream come true.

In Jack London's *The Star Rover,* Ed Worrell has precognitive dreams of a woman he eventually meets and marries. It is tough to identify a contemporaneous psi link that could cause this event. However, through telepathy Ed may have sensed their compatibility and her conscious or subconscious knowledge that she would be in the same place as he a few years later. Was this prediction out of the blue, or was it a subconscious assessment of various path-intersection probabilities based on his psi sensing of her current knowledge or expectations? It may be that through psi sensing we are all subconsciously scanning, searching for clues about our possible future paths.

I have had many precognitive dreams about future news stories, including details of photographs that have accompanied the article. When the dreams have occurred a few days ahead of the publication of the story, I may have accessed the knowledge and the intent of the writer. During those days, many publication-decision steps would have taken place and identifying a psi link at the time of the dream becomes difficult. The key event may not have occurred at the time of the dream. However, intentions may have been developing that would eventually lead to the occurrence and the future article.

It does not matter to the dreamer to what extent a precognitive dream can be traced to a contemporary root cause. Nonetheless, the experience is still precognitive to him or her. That is its value. We catch a glimpse of a future intent or incident from somewhere or someone. The event may be a certainty, a probability, or only a possibility. It may not occur at all if something goes awry in how we subconsciously assessed the probable future at the time of the dream. Unless a correction dream—an update premonition—is experienced, we never know what that odd dream was about or why it did not come to pass.

Finally, a few precognitive dreams defy any rational root-cause tracing; they just happened. Something synchronistic—something truly out of the blue—occurs. Are such events intimations of some larger pattern, a greater knowledge source?

To me, the most puzzling of all psi experiences is precognition. Sometimes it seems we have accessed, via psi, someone's current knowledge or intent. At other times, the precognitive process must have taken into consideration knowledge or intentions from many different people. That precognitive event was the result of a complex chain of events with many variables. Linking decisions may not yet have been made by many people. The event may have resulted from complex natural interactions, unpredictable equipment failure, or combinations of these. Examples would be precognition of next month's stock market status or of an earthquake with accurate timing and location information. Successful laboratory experiments in precognition, where no one knows the target to be selected, suggest possible psi access of the target's complex electronic-selection process.

Complex precognitive events suggest that some type of superconsciousness may exist that has a role in event prediction based on all possible event-generating and influencing sources. If so, this could be similar to C. G. Jung's notion of a collective unconscious, but with a psi data–integration feature. If we are all interconnected, as psi indicates, then the possibility of an integrating superconscious is not farfetched. This concept is not inconsistent with the concept of a mind hologram. Like an ordinary hologram, any portion of an individual-mind hologram would contain the same information as the larger hologram that encompasses many minds.

Years ago I had an incredibly disturbing dream about a midair collision. It was extraordinarily vivid. Toward the end of the dream, while still in that ill-fated aircraft, I became aware that I was dreaming. I was now experiencing a lucid dream. I did not want to remain on-board. My perspective shifted to outside the airplane and I saw it crash near a high mountain. A nearby airplane that was involved flew away. Then I saw a headline from the *Denver Post* that described the crash. When I woke up, I anxiously wondered if it symbolized the crash of one of my projects, or if that was a premonition of a tragic incident. One week later, a midair collision occurred near Colorado Springs, ninety miles south of Denver. One plane crashed, leaving no survivors; the other plane landed safely.

A week before that midair collision, I had decided to explore precognitive dreaming. I focused on that intent frequently throughout the day, hoping the anticipated dream would have specific information and be about an event that would make the news. I set a time limit: The dream of an event had to occur within one week. Otherwise I might forget about the dream or by chance encounter something similar to the dream simply by waiting long enough.

This dream was very likely a premonition. The details were specific and unique and it occurred within the time window I had desired for experiencing a precognitive dream. But how could such a dream have occurred? A midair catastrophe is impossible to predict through known means. No one at the time of the dream knew it would happen. I could not have sensed it from someone's current conscious knowledge or intent.

Maybe some subtle psychodynamic in the mind of one of the pilots—

some hidden, self-destructive wish—was in play. Perhaps he unconsciously flew into the wrong pattern or unconsciously ignored control-tower communications. Was this an accident looking for a place to happen? Such musings illustrate how far we must stretch in order to find root causes for impossible-to-predict premonitions.

In order to continue my study of psi dreams, including precognitive ones, I had to remain open to the possibility of them and seek them. The question was how to do this and get feedback in a consistent, timely basis?

One evening an idea came to me. Why not dream about the "Far Side" cartoon that I would see the next morning in the *Washington Post?* This cartoon would then be public knowledge for many people to see. Gary Larson, the cartoonist, certainly would know what it would be, and it would already be on press by the time I went to bed. I would have quick feedback—all I'd need to do would be pick up the morning paper on my way to work. Should I succeed in dreaming the next day's "Far Side," I could not be sure if I had sensed the cartoon in press by a process similar to remote viewing, or if I had accessed knowledge about the cartoon from someone at the *Washington Post,* or possibly Gary Larson himself. Maybe I would have perceived, via precognition, my own future knowledge when I looked at the cartoon the following morning. I was not sure how to label such an experience and it did not matter. If it worked, some type of psi event would have occurred and it would be a convenient way to practice psi. Cartoon targets, I suspected, would invoke humorous dreams. Maybe my dreams would be funnier than some of his cartoons! A laughing start in the morning could only help me cope with the traffic during my commute into Washington.

On nights when I intended to dream the "Far Side" cartoon, some dreams were clearly different from my typical ones. I could easily identify which ones related to the cartoon target. The dream figures were often distorted and surreal, very similar to the actual dream characters. The dream dynamics were highly unusual and often made no sense.

Sometimes I woke up laughing, though I recalled hardly any dream fragments. Sometimes I dreamed the cartoon sketches but missed the context or punchline. Occasionally the dream was humorous when the cartoon did not seem to be. Other times, my dream turned a clearly humorous cartoon into something serious. Consistent with findings from remote viewing research, I seemed to have accessed the cartoon shapes and forms but not the content or meaning. This makes me suspect I was not relying on telepathy or precognition of my future knowledge for perceiving the cartoons. There were times my dreams had no correlation to the target. I was either way off that night, or perhaps I found the cartoon disturbing and blocked it.

Here's an example of my psi-dream adventures into "The Far Side":

I am in a very dark place, which then becomes lively. In front of me is a small, tilted, rectangular trough—some type of game. I am surprised to see black and white balls roll down the trough. Some of them have irregular shapes. The object of the game is to play with the balls, get them to run through the wooden trough, and then accumulate them in a pile. Their irregular shapes cause odd dynamics. Gradually I have managed to stack them up and they take the shape of a huge, round pile. There are thousands of little balls.

This dream made no sense. It didn't seem funny. I was quite serious in carrying out this ball-stacking game. Wasn't this supposed to be a humorous experience? It had no sense of meaning, other than simply creating a large pile of odd-looking, black and white marbles or irregularly shaped balls.

When I arrived at Hay George's deli that morning, I speedily filled my coffee cup, grabbed the paper, dropped my seventy-eight cents on the counter, and dashed out. In the car I quickly opened to the comics. Another moment of truth. What devious twist of mind had Larson taken this time? I glanced at the cartoon and was pleasantly surprised.

Fortunately, I was totally wrong on the nature of the small black and white balls. The cartoon depicted a dark jungle scene with two naturalists standing next to a huge mound of small skulls and thin bones! They looked like shrunken heads and covered half the picture area. In the background a dark forest was composed of trees that gave the appearance of troughs or paths. My dream had created a game by having one of the wide trees serve as a path for the small black and white marbles. My pile sketch resembled the cartoon's mound of skulls.

I could see why my subconscious psi-dream maker only went half-way. I could deal with lots of small, round objects, but I may have had trouble with skulls and shrunken heads. The cartoon was captioned "The Secret Chipmunk Burial Ground."

For awhile, that's how I started off my day. Someday I'll send a note to Gary Larson and tell him about my advance glimpses of his wonderful—weird—cartoons.

Overall, my psi adventures into the "Far Side" cartoons were enjoyable. The anticipation of looking at those cartoons and comparing them to my dreams was like opening Christmas presents. More people should consider the cartoon sources as psi targets for a morning eye-opener. They would certainly lighten up the heavy atmosphere taken on by some psi researchers and quite a few of the psi practitioners that I know.

12
You Go and I'll Stay

MY ACCEPTANCE OF VALIDITY OF PSI PHENOMENA WAS CYCLICAL. WHILE MY scientific background and the attitudes of many colleagues kept pressing down hard to debunk my new findings, the traces of psi that were trying to emerge from caverns deep within my own mind were becoming convincing.

How could I deny the magician, silver-shell, or tall-black-figure dream experiences? Those were not traces—they were clear, distinct tracks. But even deep tracks can disappear quickly. They lose their shape in soft sand or snow, they are buffeted by wind, eroded by rain, or stepped on by others. They become only faint traces, then they disappear. When they are gone from sight, the tracker can only hope to find new traces. Faint traces can be followed until a better print is found. Then, carefully, the tracker can approach the den and discover the nature of whatever created the track.

My first wilderness challenge, during my early teens, was tracking animals along meadow streams and in forests. At times I can still vividly recall those piercing winter winds and my delight in discovering faint tracks in drifting snow. Similarly, memories fade and doubt sifts debris over the trail. The earlier tracks I had found were fading. I needed new tracks. I had to keep finding them to strengthen my confidence and resist the nay-sayers.

I continued exploring psi. Sometimes I worked with others, sometimes alone. Working alone had advantages. I was not bound to someone else's schedule and could try psi experiments whenever I was in the mood to do so. I could retreat to the comfort of my secure basement or bedroom. All I had to do was be sure the psi targets could not be known to me by any subliminal impression and that they could be anything. I had to keep my analytical, engineering mentality on the sidelines. No guessing. Only the psi facts would do. Analysis could come later.

One evening I felt the need to go tracking. Something kept forcing me to continue searching the wilderness for signs. That evening, I walked to a nearby forest near the Beavercreek High School. Walking softly over narrow, winding trails, I searched for tracks. Outdoor (animal) tracking helped me focus on my desire to pursue internal tracking in my consciousness—to look for psi traces or, if fortunate, psi tracks. The more I walked, the calmer I felt. My breathing, all my movements, seemed to be in synchronization. I felt at peace, comforted by the beauty of this natural space. A soft breeze shifted around glittering leaves. A stream trickled over pebbles and dropped into a clear pool, creating faint ripples. I felt calm, completely at ease with the natural world outside—and within—myself. I could now reach out, unafraid. I could now begin exploring again, to look for new psi tracks. Suddenly I noticed fresh tracks in the gravel bank of the stream. A raccoon had been there recently to drink or to find food. I followed its trail until it disappeared into thick leaves.

Returning refreshed, I felt eager to continue psi tracking and set up a new psi target. Though now calm and relaxed, my thoughts stayed with wilderness memories. It was futile to resist, I was enjoying them too much. I suspected my reminiscences would interfere with my psi perception and felt it best to search for psi tracks in my dream landscapes. I had selected a target envelope at random from a set of previously prepared sealed packages. As always, I knew nothing of their contents. The envelope was from a set of magazine targets that could be on any topic. Someone had inserted a marker, without opening the magazine, somewhere within its hundreds of pages. The page facing that marker was my intended target.

Shortly before drifting asleep, I recreated that wonderful feeling of connectedness I had felt during my forest walk. Then I shifted focus to a strong intent for dreaming that target page. I fell asleep quickly.

Many surprising, puzzling, disturbing dreams came that night. I woke up after each one and jotted down notes on my bedside pad.

The first was vague and brief.

It is dark. I am on a long journey with a small group of
explorers, whom I do not recognize. Something delays our

travel and I become frustrated, wanting to keep moving. Suddenly, intense panic surges through me. I am not sure why. Someone gives me clothing I do not want.

I woke feeling that dream panic deeply. Filled with anxiety, puzzled at the dream, I had difficulty returning to sleep. Eventually I drifted off but soon woke from another brief dream.

I see a strange mound that seems to be made of tinfoil. It is powerful, appears to be human, and moves slowly. It wears something that looks like a large, white dunce's hat. Suddenly, the mound stops moving.

I woke puzzled. This dream made no sense and seemed to bear no connection with the previous one. I felt no disturbing emotion, however, and quickly fell asleep once again. Shortly after, I awoke from this deeply troubling dream:

I am in the radio room of a large ship that seems to be on an exploration journey that happened a long time ago. I suddenly know I need to transmit an urgent message. Timing is supercritical. Desperately I try to send it out; to tell someone where we are.

When I woke, I was filled with the desperation and panic I felt in the dream. I tried to grasp the dream's significance and reviewed it over and over. What could it mean? Was something wrong with me? I puzzled over the dream and had forgotten about that target in the sealed envelope. At 3:00 AM, I awoke, startled, from a fourth dream. This time, the dream took on a sagalike quality, and I lay still for several minutes to recall details.

I am desperately trying to assemble several people whom I am boarding on a small boat. They are to begin a sailing journey and I want them to depart as soon as possible. Chaos erupts! Everyone is confused. I grab a young woman and push her toward the boat. It is her first journey and she is extremely reluctant to go along. She wants to back out of this sailing venture and stay with me. I feel intense pressure to get the small boat underway and I become very angry at her. We begin to argue, then we shout at one another. I must get her on-board! I shove her down, onto the boat—someone on-board helps restrain her. Suddenly, she leans forward and stares directly at me. With tear-filled eyes, she defies my order and shouts: "I do not want to go!" Intense, unbearable sadness sweeps through me. I know what I must do. With all my energy, I force her back...then quickly look away.

That was a powerful dream. The terrifying episode, tragic as it seemed, had transformed from a nightmare of anxiety and panic into something strangely wonderful. Even though I was very cruel to that woman, the more I reviewed it, the deeper I felt the power of her tear-filled eyes. She wanted to stay with me. That was the message of the dream. I felt deeply an intense love bond with her, one that tore my heart and soul apart when I forced her away. That was the feeling that stayed with me as I reviewed, or relived, the dream. No longer filled with anxiety and panic, I fell into a peaceful sleep.

The next morning, I grabbed my notes and hurried to the local coffee shop where I recorded the dreams in my journal. It was a workday and I did not have time to analyze what they were about, but the dreams were on my mind all day and at times I had difficulty concentrating. The power of that ending lingered, and I did not see how it would ever go away. I did not want it to.

That evening, I returned to my forest sanctuary to walk and to think. Fairly certain the dream series was not "of me"—unless some distant, possibly genetic, memory had surfaced—I found it more likely that the dreams were of the target. The challenge was related to the reason I loved tracking animals in the wilderness: Could I identify the creature that left those tracks? Could I identify the target picture from the traces, or tracks, it had left in my dream landscape? Now was the time for analysis and I welcomed back my engineering mind, my detective nature, my track-analyzing instincts.

I sat on a log above that stream and relived the dream sequences. If all the dreams related in some way to the target page, then they seemed inconsistent. Some of them did convey a strong feeling of frustration and panic. The first and last dreams conveyed a sense of new exploration, but the last also had a strong tragic mood.

After pondering these dreams for a long time, I decided the psi target very likely portrayed something tragic. Perhaps something from World War I or II, or an early exploration tragedy with people lost and starving in a remote area, desperately trying to get help or to escape something. The radio room of the ship and the small sailing boat clearly indicated a nautical setting. The act of sending a message for help had to be important. I was sure the intense feeling at the end of the last dream was a major clue. But exactly what was that target page about?

I did not feel I could analyze the dreams any further, yet I felt that the dreams were of the target and that the saga dream should be easily recognizable. Maybe something in my psyche still resisted psi tracking. Maybe I wanted to track, but not get too close to the hidden den.

Later that night I retrieved the target package. Slowly, anxiously, I grasped the marker, snapped the magazine open to the target page, and stared down. No matter how often I had done this, the shock was still the same. At first I could not believe the blatant truth on that page. It penetrated the layers of still-lingering resistance. I had to accept what I saw, once again.

The marker had been inserted at an article on the sinking of the *Titanic!*

Now all the dreams made sense. They had captured the essence of the article. Old black-and-white photos were very close to the dream scenes and actions. A tremendous wave of relief swept over me. The tragic dreams were not of me; my psi track-maker had been very busy throughout the night. One photo showed the inside of the *Titanic*'s stateroom. The article started by describing the impact with the iceberg and the crew's urgent radio calls for help. That distress signal was heard by the *Carpathian,* a large ship sixty miles away. It turned and steamed toward the *Titanic.* My dream of the radio room of a large ship resembled the picture of the *Titanic*'s stateroom.

The beginning of the article had a vivid description of the initial panic and confusion following the collision with the iceberg. As people were informed of the need to abandon ship, many had difficulty parting with their valuables and dress clothing before crowding into small lifeboats.

The second dream—the strange mound made of tinfoil with a hat that looked like a large, white dunce's hat—now made sense. One of the photographs showed a large, irregular-shaped iceberg on a dark sea. On the opposite side of that page was an out-of-context cartoon that happened to be in the middle of the article. Its fat figure wore a tall, white dunce's hat. When I held up the page, both the iceberg and the dunce's hat nearly overlapped. No wonder my psi tracker became confused. It was as if something had stepped on the track I was following! The idea of a massive mound stopping, of something delaying our journey, now made sense.

Again, I looked at the target page. It had a picture taken from the *Carpathian* that showed a small boat packed with nearly frozen survivors. Even though I thought of that boat as a sailboat in the dream, I had not noticed any masts or sails. The words on that page and the caption below the rescue scene were recreations of dialogue between the men and officers who stayed behind and the women and children they hurriedly loaded into the lifeboats. Some women did not want to board. They wanted to remain with their fiancés or husbands. The dialogue captures a moment when a woman is being forced on-board the lifeboat!

It was that dialogue I so vividly and dramatically recreated in my last dream. I had relived and deeply experienced that powerful moment of sacrifice, when the man, who knew he would not survive, forced away a woman who wanted to stay with him, to join him on his new journey.

I took another look at the title of the article: "You Go and I'll Stay."

Sometimes psi tracks can be too powerful, but that is a risk worth taking. How else could I ever know what sacrifices like those made by the man on that tilting deck were like? This dream experiment was far more than an interesting experience. It took me into the depths of my heart and soul.

Sometimes, in quiet moments along a mountain trail or near a gentle stream, I recall the time when that heartbroken woman with tear-filled eyes turned and asked to stay. Only a dream? I don't think so.

On the Trail of Synchronicity

The philosophical principle that underlies our conception of natural law is *causality*.... The connection of events may in certain circumstances be other than casual, and require another principle of explanation.

➤ C. G. Jung, *Synchronicity: An Acausal Connecting Principle* (page 5)

Many demands fill our lives—family, society, vocation. We may have inner promptings toward new activities, for uncovering talents, or for personal or transpersonal understanding. Most of the time, we can receive assistance from a variety of sources; printed material, electronic links, or directly from others. Sometimes, however, we can't locate what is needed or we are not sure where to begin looking.

In these situations, synchronicity can give us a helping hand. Synchronicities are unpredictable experiences that bring us into contact with the information that we need or the insights that we seek. They seem to occur out of the blue, as unusual, chance occurrences. However, they are not due to chance. A subconscious process has nudged our paths or the paths of others into a meaningful intersection. They differ from chance occurrences due to their uniqueness, their meaning, and the feelings or emotions they evoke. These meaningful arrangements help us discover what we need to know.

The tests are need and timing.

Synchronicities are dynamic events that occur at surprising times in response to pressing needs or concerns. They resemble intuitions and sometimes call our attention to certain patterns or to some new insight. The purpose of such synchronicities may be to reveal deeper aspects of our nature, or to demonstrate transpersonal connectivity. Certain synchronistic events call our attention to inner promptings that motivate pursuit of new constructive and integrative life goals. Synchronistic experiences remind us there is much we do not yet understand about the reach of our conscious and subconscious mind.

In some instances of suspected synchronicity, the event may have been due only to chance. Other meaningful coincidences may have occurred as a result of a heightened awareness and subliminal sensitivities. We are more alert and sense subtle clues that help us discover the needed information. Genetic patterns can bring about behavioral similarities and identical interests between family members that seem synchronistic, but are not. Identical twins separated at birth often have remarkable correlation in their lives, as they discover when reunited. The psi process, however, appears to be the basic principle behind most synchronistic events.

When we consider synchronicity to be linked with psi phenomena, we can take an active role in experiencing synchronicities more frequently. We can call on our inner communication pathway, our psi talents, for a synchronistic helping hand in times of need.

As for any psi task, the prerequisite for opening up to this extra hand is having a specific goal and a strong motivation or intent to achieve that goal. As we do whatever we can to accomplish that goal, our intent is reinforced. Our commitment to that goal, that need, signals out to the subconscious levels of others, no matter where they are. An inner dynamics is set in motion that can, within practical constraints, bring about an unplanned, meaningful intersection of paths.

We may find something lost or hidden that we need; we may meet someone who has a piece of the puzzle that can help us achieve our goal. When that event occurs, we may experience a sense of déjà vu or be strangely puzzled. The experience of these helping-hand situations is an indication that synchronicity is at work. We have had an encounter with a meaningful coincidence that we know was not an incident of blind chance.

When we open to them, synchronicities can help us in a variety of situations, ranging from major to minor. Our psi network can respond to all needs, the great and the small. It is ready to help us if we are open, receptive, and flexible. Sometimes our psi talents can help us avoid undesirable situations. We may be nudged through subconscious impulses into a wrong turn only to discover later that an accident had occurred on our intended route. We may miss an appointment then find out after the fact that it was in our best interest not to have met with the other people. These can be seen as a type of synchronicity: We received help in the form of avoidance, which may have arisen due to our basic survival needs and instincts.

Similarly, we may be drawn into unpleasant situations if we focus too strongly on negative or destructive desires. Our natural self-preservation instincts might be overcome. Synchronicity follows a like-attracts-like principle. Either good or not-so-good situations can occur depending on the intensity and polarity of our sincere desires.

Sometimes we receive hints of approaching synchronicities. We find their tracks in our psi landscape in the form of a hunch that something important is about to happen or a vaguely remembered precognitive dream about that approaching intersection. When the meaningful event happens, we may not be sure if it was synchronistic or precognitive but the distinction doesn't really matter. They are different facets of our psi diamond. Sometimes precognition gives us a warning of an out-of-context, unexpected event so that we may take evasive action. Other precognitive alerts may come in the form of progress reports on how our intently held goal is about to be given a helping hand. They make us more alert and receptive to potential synchronicities, which is especially important if the intersection window is open only briefly.

More than the intersection may need to occur. For example, when we come to the eventful "place" or are near the "attractor" object or person, we need to pay attention, to take a closer look, to say an impulsive, "Hello." The meaning of the crossing paths can then be discovered. Unfortunately, there are times we are like two ships passing in a foggy night. Ripples in the darkness toss hints that something is out there, but we quietly pass by making no contact, receiving no information.

Many times in our lives synchronicities come close but pass by unfulfilled. By being more alert to our hunches, being more spontaneous, and by recalling dreams, synchronicities in our lives will increase. All we need to do is remain flexible and explore for ourselves. We also must expect them to happen. Accept that helping hand—for both the great and the small—as a natural part of our lives. Then we are better prepared to catch their traces, find their tracks.

A female client of Carl Jung, the well-known dreamwork pioneer, had a dream of a beetle, which is often cited as an example of synchronicity. However, it can also be seen as a precognitive dream. In her dream, "someone had given her a golden scarab—a costly piece of jewelry." The next day, during her meeting with Jung, while she was still telling the dream, a similar green-gold beetle, rare at that time of year, flew against the window. To Jung, in the context of the on-going therapy, that dream and the appearance of the live scarabaeid beetle proved to be a pivotal point in the woman's analysis. They led to new understanding for both the client and psychiatrist. The unexpected real beetle had significance far beyond the apparent unusual coincidence. Jung saw this episode as synchronistic and was less interested in the precognitive, psi aspect.

The event led the woman to relax her rigid views and to accept her own spontaneous creative nature, which she had so rigidly suppressed. In Egyptian mythology, a scarab symbolized the soul and rebirth. The dreamer either sensed the future appearance of the beetle, or she subconsciously influenced it so that it arrived at the window at a meaningful time, thereby helping Jung and herself fulfill her greatest need—a breakthrough in therapy. He had been intensely focused on "the hope that something unexpected and irrational would turn up, something which would burst the intellectual retort into which she had sealed herself." (C. G. Jung, *Synchronicity: An Acausal Connecting Principle*, p. 109)

Or did Jung attract the event? Previously he had exhibited psi talent. In *Memories, Dreams, and Reflections,* he describes his psi dreams and synchronistic experiences. One precognitive dream had unusual details of a house he had not yet seen but later visited. Other dreams ranged from future personal incidents to a forewarning of World War II, which did not begin until several years later. Perhaps, through their subconscious connection, his strong intention for therapy resolution resonated with the client's dream process and facilitated her precognitive dream. Perhaps he subconsciously influenced the spontaneous flight of the beetle that day. This event, and other meaningful coincidences he observed, led him to develop the concept of synchronicity as an acausal principle that operates independent of time and space.

Jung coined the term *synchronicity,* which he considered to be a fundamental property of mind—or psyche—and matter that had no cause-and-effect mechanism. Eventually he collaborated with quantum physics pioneer Wolfgang Pauli and expanded this concept. Jung considered psi phenomena to be examples of acausal or synchronistic events. However, others interpret synchronistic events that call our attention to deep inner prompting as being independent of our psi nature.

I believe that our psi nature reveals a process that is fundamental to all synchronistic events. Synchronicity is deeply rooted in the psi process. I was first alerted to the possibility of meaningful coincidences in 1954, as described in the first chapter in this section, "Synchronicity for a Dime." It took many years and many synchronicities before I could accept them as more than mere chance events. Exploring psi by working with remote viewing and psi dreams led me to consider synchronicities as psi-mediated events. Once I became alert to their traces, I recognized that synchronicities occurred frequently. Sometimes they came out of the blue in response to a clear need; sometimes precognitive dreams alerted me to their approach. There is much we do not know about psi, synchronicity, and the nature of the universe, but lack of understanding does not mean we cannot be open to synchronicities and the help they can provide.

13
Synchronicity for a Dime

IN THE SUMMER OF 1954, BETWEEN MY SOPHOMORE AND JUNIOR YEARS AT Pennsylvania State University, I received an invitation to attend the wedding of a classmate's sister. The prospect of traveling from my parents' home near Reading, Pennsylvania, to his home city, several hundred miles away, loomed before me as an exciting adventure. This would be my first long, solo trip driving my father's car. Being on my own, driving, and taking part in a party-filled weekend generated a heightened sense of anticipation and excitement. Responsibility for the car and my own conduct seemed overwhelming.

Many issues concerned me. Since I was from a rural area, I was unfamiliar with driving in city traffic and wasn't looking forward to that aspect of the journey—there were no beltways at that time. Since I was on a tight budget (that is, almost broke), I had to be very careful how I spent what little cash I had during the anticipated partying. With two more years at Penn State, I could afford no frills; certainly no expensive dates.

As the weekend approached, my concerns evaporated and I eagerly headed off as if embarking on a great adventure. The weekend was soon over, and the adventure I had anticipated did not occur. The bride and groom hit and ran; there was no wedding reception blast or late-night party. Something else happened, however, that has stayed with me over the years. Very disappointed and in a depressed mood, I began my return home early that Sunday.

Since I left the city earlier than planned, I chose a long route back home. I filled the gas tank at least one time. The weather was great and driving was a pleasure. Traffic was light. I explored seacoast towns I had never visited and had an expensive seafood meal, a rare treat for someone from Pennsylvania Dutch–farming country. Slowly daydreams and fantasies returned. Maybe the next wedding would be more interesting; maybe as a junior I would have more of a social life. I was becoming very tired of my engineering program. My interests had been shifting to psychology and the humanities, but there was no way to explore them at this time. How could I switch my curriculum at such a late stage?

My daydreams during the long drive home became longer and longer and my attention drifted wildly. Suddenly, I became aware of the gas tank gauge. The needle was touching the big *E*. I had to fill up in order to reach home. When I pulled into a nearby gas station, I discovered that I only had twenty cents—not quite enough for a gallon of gas in 1954 and certainly not enough to buy gas for the long drive home. I sat in the car, considering my options. I rejected the thought of trying to borrow a few dollars from strangers. I searched the car, streets, and sidewalks, even checked the coin-return slot on pay phones, hoping to find change, but found nothing.

I was north of Philadelphia, near Bristol. As I strolled around, I recalled that a college classmate, Jack Anderson, lived in Bristol, so I decided to drive into the city a few miles away, check the telephone directory, and call him. He would enjoy my surprise visit and would be glad to loan me a few dollars for gas.

I drove to the center of Bristol, found a pay phone that still had a directory attached, and paged to the Andersons. My great idea quickly turned to folly. There were more than fifty Andersons and I had no way to sort them. Maybe Jack was named after his father. There was a Jack Anderson listed. Anxiously, I dropped one of my two dimes into the telephone coin slot and dialed. The party that answered did not have a son named Jack. Now I was down to my last dime. It was late and a sense of panic began to creep through me. I had to admit to the real possibility of being stranded; of being stuck in a strange city with only one thin dime. It was not a good feeling.

I noticed a police station across the street. Maybe Jack had a traffic violation and the police could find records with his home phone number. With great trepidation, I approached the police chief and explained my plight. He checked the files, but did not find a Jack Anderson.

I still could make one more call. Could I somehow blindly choose the right Anderson from those fifty names? At first I felt it could be possible, but as I approached the phone booth, something strange happened. I had a sudden strong feeling that my idea could not work. There was no point in trying and I quickly walked away from the telephone. Ahead was a diner, and I found myself aimlessly entering and ordering a cup of coffee. This was totally irrational. I at least had a slim chance of reaching Jack if I made a random telephone call with that remaining dime.

I sat at the counter slowly sipping my one-and-only cup of coffee. I saw no way to leave Bristol and had no idea what to do next. Yet, as I sipped that delicious cup of coffee, I felt unusually calm, as if I had nothing to be concerned about. I should have been in some sort of panic mode but was not.

Since it was now early evening, the diner had filled with customers. I remained seated at the counter, slowly stirring and sipping, occasionally glancing into the kitchen. The aroma of hot, delicious food wafted around. I felt pangs of hunger.

Then, inexplicably, I felt a great need to leave. The counter was not full, and the waitress had not hinted at my stay being overlong. I quickly got up, fished out that remaining dime, and moved into the line in front of the cash register. Almost immediately an elderly couple stepped behind me and others lined up behind them. As I approached the cashier, I suddenly had a strong urge to turn around and ask that elderly couple a question.

"Excuse me, but do you by any chance know a Jack Anderson, who is in the aeronautical engineering program at Penn State?"

I felt awkward with such an abrupt style, especially with strangers in a strange city. My question, surprisingly, had impact. They both seemed taken aback. After a few moments, the man, somewhat shaken, said, "Why, yes. Jack is my nephew! How do you know that we know Jack?"

They both gazed at me wide-eyed. I felt a slight shock go through me, probably similar to theirs when I had suddenly turned and asked about Jack.

Good question. How *did* I know? Why did I step in line at the moment when they would be immediately behind me?

After I explained my situation, they invited me to return to the booth they had just left. It had not yet been cleared for the next customers. They were curious and wanted to talk. After we introduced ourselves—Harry and Edith, as I recall—they continued to ask why I talked to *them* rather than anyone else in the diner about Jack. I had no answer. I told them all I was trying to do was find Jack Anderson.

"This is hard to believe," said Harry, still in mild shock. "Edith and I are on our way to the Andersons. We only visit them a few times a year. You can follow us to their place. I'll call ahead and let Jack know you are coming along."

I knew that Harry intended to verify my connection with Jack. After all, I was a stranger and may have been setting them up. When he returned from the pay phone, he was shaking his head, and frowning.

"Jack was there and said, 'Great, come on over!' He can't believe you just happened to bump into us. I still can't believe it either," he said.

"What is surprising to me," said Edith, "is that this is the first time we have been in this diner. We hardly ever go to downtown Bristol."

"This is my first visit to Bristol, and I'm sure glad you chose this diner this evening," I said.

We chatted about the Penn State Nittany Lions and the classes Jack and I were in together. Harry bought me a meal that I devoured. As I was sipping my second cup of coffee, Harry glanced up and asked, "Did you say you came into Bristol to look up the Andersons in the phone book?"

"Yes. The student directory lists Bristol as Jack's home city," I replied.

"Well, then," he said, with a deep frown, "I need to tell you something. You are in the wrong city. The Andersons moved north of here about two years ago and are no longer carried in the Bristol phone book."

A very humble person emerged from that silver East Coast diner that evening, slowly following an elderly couple to Jack's place. Jack and I had lots to talk about. His parents loaned me enough money for gas to return home that night.

To this day, I often relive that strange experience when one last, thin dime bought a cup of coffee—and time—and helped set up a startling intersection of paths.

14
A Good Seat Assignment

THE SYNCHRONICITY FOR A DIME EXPERIENCE MADE ME AWARE OF MEANINGFUL coincidences and led me to ponder the nature of mind. Eventually I directed more spare time to reading the psychology and philosophy literature and took a few graduate courses on these topics. I remained in my engineering/physics profession. However, I held hope of somehow making a transition into activities more closely related to the psychological than my current work with physical phenomena and analysis permitted. When I became connected with the SRI remote viewing research, I had the opportunity to pursue both physical science and psychological interests professionally.

As I continued with remote viewing research, teaching "The Psychic Realm," and pursuing independent psi dream exploration, I frequently experienced spontaneous psi events and synchronicities. My wilderness travels and growing interest in the natural world may have generated feelings helpful for synchronistic occurrences as well. Some of these synchronicities helped me in my personal life. Others related to my remote viewing activities and emerging Stargate responsibilities. A few of them helped me in other professional duties that I continued to hold. In many instances, when a pressing personal or professional need arose, something unexpected would happen that provided insight or help. Some of these synchronicities occurred when traveling. Keeping a journal of my activities and experiences provided a method to identify their occurrences more easily.

One of my additional duties in the mid-1970s, during the initial phase of the Stargate project, was as chairman of a technical group that examined radar and optical sensor data. My background in these topics was very general, and I had much to learn. Since reading technical reports and meeting with knowledgeable colleagues was not sufficient, I arranged visits with leading experts and invited them to present papers at my technical-group meetings.

One specific topic was troublesome to me and I needed more information than was readily available. Dr. B., an expert from a distant research facility, was recommended as a consultant. In an attempt to set up a meeting, we played telephone tag for several weeks. An important conference was approaching; I wanted his input concerning the agenda and hoped he could present a technical paper as well. With only a few weeks remaining, and no contact, not even a response to my letters, it looked like I would not have his assistance for my conference.

Then an unexpected business trip came up that took me from my home area in Beavercreek, Ohio, to Washington, D.C., and Florida. After completing my business in Washington, I caught a flight for Florida from National Airport that routed through Atlanta. It was a rush hour flight and all seats were taken. I was late making reservations and was fortunate to have gotten a seat.

After leveling off at our cruising altitude, I relaxed and began writing in my journal. The man sitting next to me read intently. Occasionally I glanced at the reports he held, wondering if I could catch a glimpse of the topic that held his interest so strongly. I did not want to be too obvious and could not see what he was reading.

In time, the flight attendant brought snacks. As my seat companion placed his reading material in a briefcase, I saw the title of one of the reports. It was on optical-signature data!

Could it be? Could my seat companion be an expert on the topic I needed to learn more about? Maybe I could obtain help from him and give up trying to contact Dr. B.

Long flights are especially productive for creative thinking and developing new approaches to projects. Therefore, I usually resist talking to strangers on airplanes, especially when they are busy and look preoccupied. I prefer to read or write. But this flight seemed different. As we were finishing our snacks, I turned to him and said: "Excuse me, but I think we may have a common interest. Did I catch a glimpse of something about optics on the title of that paper? I happen to be chairman of such a group, and..."

Pausing, I hoped he would pick up the conversation. Quickly he turned toward me. Squinting through his thick glasses, he replied, "Yes, I do know a little about such things."

After I introduced myself, he handed me his business card, smiling. I gazed at the name in disbelief. This was Dr. B.!

By the time we landed in Atlanta where he transferred flights, I had received a tutorial on his specialty and he had given me advice concerning conference agenda topics. He also agreed to give a presentation at his first opportunity—if not at my upcoming meeting, then the next. I accomplished more on that flight than I could have with phone calls or letters and it saved me an extra business trip.

Although blind chance may be the explanation some would use for our encounter, I had my doubts. A synchronistic-timing coordinator was probably at work somewhere deep in our psyches. I had a specific need at that time. We both were traveling and somehow our arrangements intersected. From hundreds of possible pairings, we were assigned adjacent seats.

Many people have been in the right place at the right time and have experienced similar synchronicities. Travel can facilitate meaningful coincidences. We are in contact with more people; we may be more relaxed and feel free from pressing demands. Travel generates a mood of spontaneity that I suspect has a strong hand in nudging different paths into a meaningful intersection.

While any single meaningful coincidence cannot make a case for synchronicity, such occurrences over time strengthen that possibility. Some chance encounters that appear to be synchronistic will probably occur. However, the degree of uniqueness of a current need and the timing of the event is a clue for differentiating between chance and synchronicity.

The case for synchronistic events is strengthened by laboratory findings. The demonstration of psi in a laboratory setting, where conditions are generally inflexible and may feel unnatural, makes a strong case for the reality of naturally occurring, spontaneous psi experiences. Synchronicity can be seen as a psi-mediated event similar to some instances of intuition.

While the psi mechanism appears to be acausal, and has yet to be understood, some psychological correlates with psi success in laboratory situations have been identified. High motivation, perceived importance of the task, and interest and curiosity all contribute to success. Ability to suspend negative views toward psi, a history of spontaneous psi experiences, and flexibility in shifting perspectives from outer to inner orientation contribute to psi success. There may also be physical correlates to success due to environment, time of day, and other factors.

During travel, we may more easily slip into a psi-conducive state. We become more flexible in order to respond to planned and unplanned travel demands. The act of travel temporarily releases us from habits and patterns and can have a freeing effect on our mental processes. Our sense of creativity is higher than usual. We are—must be—open to new experiences. During travel we are more curious and probably more relaxed than at other times. We pay more attention to all our senses, thereby giving our hidden psi sense a bit more chance to break through.

When we travel, we become explorers and can expect the unexpected, including synchronicity.

15
Fast Meeting on the Metro

I WAS IN WASHINGTON, D.C., ATTENDING TO PERSONAL BUSINESS. HAVING FALLEN behind schedule toward the end of the day, I had to delay one of my visits: I had hoped to stop by the Peace Corps office to pick up information for my son and to find a point-of-contact person with whom I could discuss a new program I had heard about. It was late in the day, and I caught the Metro for a short run to the station in Virginia where I had parked my car.

The Metro was packed. I was standing near the exit door in one of the many passenger cars, squeezed in by a crowd of evening commuters en route home. The train rambled through the Potomac River tunnel, and stopped briefly at Rosslyn, Virginia. People surged out; more squeezed in. Holding onto a pole, I kept my balance as the train snapped and swayed toward my destination, when my attention was drawn to a man standing next to me. I hardly ever talk to strangers on subways—everyone is preoccupied or tired—but I felt an impulse to talk to him. Maybe it was his friendly demeanor; maybe I simply felt like talking.

"Hope you don't have to stand too long," I said cautiously, "This Metro is jammed tonight."

"Oh no," he answered in a friendly tone. "I get off at the next stop. It's a short run for me."

"Fortunately, it's a short haul for me too, but then it's a long drive home to southern Maryland," I commented.

"I don't think I could deal with these crowds on a daily basis," he replied. "I'm in here a few times a month for a meeting with the Peace Corps."

"The Peace Corps?" I asked, clearly surprised.

"Yes...why?"

"My son just came back from several years in Nepal as a Peace Corps volunteer," I replied loudly to counter the train's racket as it gained speed. "I wanted to visit the Peace Corps office today to get some reports and talk about a project I read about. I ran out of time."

I introduced myself and gave him my card.

He studied my card intently. Smiling he opened his wallet.

"Here's my card," he said, trying to keep balance as the Metro swayed suddenly. He could tell I was shocked as I quietly read his card:

```
James Graff, Consultant, Peace Corps
```

"I find this hard to believe. We both have the same last name! Our name is not that common," he said.

I glanced at him and nodded.

"You know," he said, "I hardly ever talk to anyone on the Metro. It's interesting you would strike up a conversation."

"Yes, James Graff, it is, isn't it?"

The train screeched to a halt and we braced ourselves against the pole. Quickly he gave me some contacts and asked me to call him any time. The sliding doors whooshed open. He surged away with the departing mob; more people rushed in. The doors slammed shut.

I got off at the next stop and began my long drive home, pleased by what had been accomplished in that overplanned day.

16

A Surprise in
the Caucasus

WHEN I RETIRED, I TREATED MYSELF TO AN EARTHWATCH EXPEDITION. I HAVE SUPPORTED Earthwatch since its inception and remain totally in agreement with their stated goal of providing opportunities for anyone to take part in ecological-research activities worldwide. Their projects usually last two weeks and are limited to small groups of people who are willing to get their hands dirty.

I chose a Russian activity. I wanted to see first-hand what the Russian people were like and I wanted to learn more about their ecological situation, which seemed dismal.

Then came the demands of trip preparation—travel schedules, visa approval, equipment selection. An Aeroflot connection took me from Washington to Moscow, where I joined a small group of international volunteers. We met our Russian team leader, a scientist from an institute with the Russian Academy of Sciences, and made final arrangements for our expedition to the Caucasus, a mountainous region that stretches between the Black Sea and the Caspian Sea. Nine of us were on his team—four Russians, four Americans, and one Japanese.

After arriving at Souji, a city on the Black Sea, we were taken by four-wheel drive vehicles up narrow, winding, cliff-hanging roads to our base camp several thousand feet above sea level. Our jeeps and small trucks had to ford fast-running mountain streams since the small bridges were unsafe for heavy vehicles to cross. Our camp was a lovely old stone lodge that at one time served as a retreat for high-ranking Communist-party officials.

Our mountain setting was inside the one-thousand-square-mile Kavkaz State Nature Preserve, one of the best-preserved wilderness areas on earth. For two weeks we climbed steep cliffs, measured tree sizes, and took soil samples. We monitored water flow in mountain streams and tested for various chemicals and pollutants. Since there was no reliable hot water available, we bathed in the icy mountain stream that cascaded past the lodge.

The expedition was a wonderful, exhilarating experience. I will always treasure memories of the primitive setting, the local villagers, and the nearby twelve-thousand-foot-high mountain peaks. Our team was very compatible. The Russians were great hosts and spoke good English. The rest of us struggled mightily with a few Russian words and phrases.

The days were filled with cross-country travel through thick bushes and ancient forests. Walking and carrying equipment across that steep terrain and through the dense foliage was exhausting. Hard work stressed our muscles and stretched our appetites. Evening meals consisted of delicious local Russian fare. Our camaraderie soared.

After the first week, a nagging concern crept dimly into my awareness. We had been instructed on the flora and wildlife, and on the mountain's geological and ecological character, but no one, not even the nearby residents, had mentioned anything about snakes. I couldn't believe none were in this region. While I was not particularly afraid of snakes, there might be poisonous ones present and if there were, I certainly wanted to know. The thick underbrush made it difficult to see where—or on what— our steps might fall. I was becoming concerned.

One morning, I woke recalling a vague dream about snakes. Was that my overactive imagination? I approached our expedition leader, Anatoly, and expressed my concern. He assured me that there were no snakes in that region—certainly no poisonous ones. He had been leading ecological expeditions here for several years and had never seen any sign of snakes; neither had any of his team, the local foresters, or the people nearby on the farms or in the villages. I wondered if he was saying that simply to allay my worry.

Early the second week, I started to pay more attention to where I and the others walked. Something did not seem right. Was I talking myself into a minor paranoia?

During lunch one day, I felt a sudden urge, without apparent reason, to go to the back of the building. I had walked around the lodge, and the nearby utility building, many times. At no time had I detected anything of concern. Only stray farm animals, chickens, goats, hogs, and horses wandered around. The lodge was built on a small, level clearing, very close to a steep bush- and tree-covered hill that eventually merged with a high ridge a thousand feet above. As I walked around the building, I suddenly stopped. Not knowing why, I turned and gazed into the bush-covered bank a few feet in front of me.

Directly in front of me, underneath thin branches, eyeball to eyeball, I faced a snake! I was too shocked to check the orientation of the snake's pupils—a sure way to identify a pit viper from harmless snakes. At that moment, I was not inclined toward analysis. With a speed I had not called upon in years, I raced back to the dining hall.

"Anatoly," I said, excitedly, "there is something out here you need to see. Right now!"

His curiosity piqued, he dashed outside with me. I stopped in front of the steep bank and pointed, hoping the reptile was still visible.

"Look. Look at the base of that thick bush! There's more than branches there. Do you see it?"

The snake was still there, but was now slithering a hasty retreat into some hidden hole-entrance under the leaves.

Fortunately, Anatoly caught a glimpse of it. Otherwise, my sanity may have been on the line. He stared at the disappearing snake. It was not large, and probably not a poisonous variety.

He said something in Russian I did not understand. Then, in English, "I've never seen any snake in this area before. I only caught a glimpse of it, but I don't think it is poisonous."

"Glad to hear that. But don't you see, where there is one snake, there might be—"

He got the drift. After lunch we had a long instruction on snakes. He agreed that it might be a good idea to be more alert for them. I made sure I had my emergency snakebite kit along on our future treks.

There were no more sightings after that; I had no more snake dreams. I had no sudden urges to peer into the underbrush.

I often wonder what led to my "finding" that snake. Why did I suddenly feel the urge to walk around the building, turn, and look at the precise spot where the well-camouflaged snake rested? Was it important for Anatoly to be aware of snakes in the area, possibly for his and the team's safety? Was it to resolve a nagging concern of mine—a type of hunch from a vague dream? Had I sensed it subliminally when I walked past that spot earlier? Did I reach out, via psi, to search and find? Was it synchronistic?

The snake's path and mine intersected briefly. I had a need to know and, as a result, had found what I was told could not be there.

Synchronicities occur for the great and the small. I am open and receptive to all kinds.

You never know what interesting path intersections are ahead, or around the corner.

17
Fire Drill

ON MY GET-ACQUAINTED VISIT TO SRI, IN THE SUMMER OF 1976, I WAS INVITED TO witness a remote viewing experiment. The remote viewer was Hella Hammid, with whom I had become acquainted by phone during the remote viewing experiment we dubbed "Hella's Cave."

Hal Puthoff and a colleague, the beacon people, selected at random a target site in the San Francisco Bay area—a peaceful scene near a tall, modern building, which was surrounded by a large plaza with well-tended landscaping. The two men slowly walked around the plaza, hoping that Hella—who was sequestered in the SRI lab several miles away—could describe the key features of the site and sketch the tall building at its center. The weather was comfortable and the sky clear that afternoon. A few people strolled past as Hal wandered around gazing at the scene and absorbing the serenity of the site.

As the thirty-minute session neared completion, all hell broke loose. Alarms sounded; people streamed from the building and filled the plaza. In seconds, Hal and his colleague had become surrounded and squeezed by the large crowd. Sirens sounded loudly as fire trucks roared into the plaza and screeched to a halt, their red, flashing lights pulsing and reflecting from nearby windows. Fire fighters ran from their trucks into the building. A few minutes later, the fire-fighters returned to their trucks and drove away. There had been no fire; it was only a drill. The crowd meandered back into the building. Shortly after the trucks departed, Hal and his companion returned to the SRI laboratory to see how Hella had done.

By the time they returned, Hella's notes and sketches had been photocopied and logged into project files. I was with Hella and Russ when Hal entered the remote viewing room.

"All right, you guys, what happened?" Hella asked, looking perplexed. "I was sitting here, quietly sketching and relaxing, when suddenly I see a mob! An angry mob! They were bumping all around you!...Was that some type of frenzied fire drill?"

Hal seemed to be in mild shock, and several moments passed before he explained to Hella what had happened.

Her sketch of the building was quite good, too.

That fire drill provided a unique insight. Hal had told me that remote viewers usually did well describing static targets such as lakes, mountains, or structures. Many of the previous targets did have incidental nearby activity such as heavy traffic, moving trains, or walking people. The viewers for these projects rarely sensed or reported them and consequently he did not believe they could reliably detect or identify activity at a target site.

In this experiment, Hella demonstrated that detecting motion and determining its nature was possible. To Hella, the excitement and action at that site were like beacons flashing in the night. This was the first time in hundreds of experiments that a fire drill had occurred while the beacon people were at the target area. It had taken the unexpected occurrence of a fire drill while Hella was the remote viewer to challenge Hal's belief that motion could not accurately be detected.

I suspect that not every remote viewer would have perceived the surge of people or sensed the nature of the activity. Some cognitive styles are structural, or form-driven, and therefore place less focus on motion or emotion. Hella had previously done well in sensing moods and feelings associated with the target area. Motion and emotion at the target area may have had similar effects on her.

This incident struck me as meaningful—as synchronistic—much like a psychotherapeutic session I had read about in which the client's dream material taught the doctor a lesson. I thought of this event frequently, but didn't discuss my view of its synchronicity for seventeen years.

In August 1993, I attended a Parapsychological Association conference in Toronto. This lovely Canadian city is safe for walking, even at odd hours, and I frequently took advantage of this opportunity and especially liked to stroll around the streets late at night and shortly after dawn. One morning, toward the end of the conference, I was joined by another early walker, Dr. Robert Morris. We strolled around near our hotel rather haphazardly.

Bob holds the University of Edinburgh's Koestler Chair of Parapsychology, which was established through an endowment established by the British writer Arthur Koestler, who had a strong interest in ESP and synchronistic experiences. The first book I read on synchronicity was his, *The Roots of Coincidence*.

As we walked, Bob and I discussed the significance of emotional events and their role in facilitating the psi process and the latest psi research. My thoughts drifted back to Hella's fire drill many years earlier. I knew that Bob was interested in synchronistic experiences and I wondered if he would see it as an example of synchronicity.

Just as I finished telling about Hella's fire drill experience, we came to a large public school. Suddenly, our concentration was broken by the sound of sirens approaching. Police cars or ambulances seemed to be racing up the main street two blocks behind us but we paid little attention and continued walking. The sounds grew louder. Several vehicles turned the corner and raced down the street we were on, screeching to a halt just where we were standing—they were fire trucks! Fire-fighters jumped from them and ran into the school. In seconds, other trucks arrived, but no one left them. Intense red lights continued to flash. Anxiously, we stared at the school, expecting to see smoke and fire, but we saw nothing unusual. No fire alarms sounded from the school. Since it was early, no students were present. I suspected a false alarm or a test had occurred. In a few minutes, the fire-fighters emerged from the school and casually milled around the trucks. We asked what was happening. "Nothing to worry about," said the closest one, "this is only a drill."

We lingered a few moments and then began our return to the hotel.

I knew Bob was as curious as I about Hella's incident and our timely discussion of it. Why should I have talked to Bob about it at that exact time? I had met him frequently during the conference and could have mentioned it anytime. Perhaps I had faintly, or subliminally, heard those sirens when they were distant, which influenced me to think of fires. However, I had frequently heard sirens of all kinds during the week and was accustomed to them. What about our location and timing? Of the many possible routes we could have chosen, why did we pass this school just as the fire trucks arrived? Was the pairing of our discussion of Hella's incident and the fire drill also a synchronistic event? Did we have this experience to better appreciate the significance of a similar one seventeen years prior?

We discussed Hella's fire drill as a meaningful experience for Hal. He had a need for observing an experience like a fire drill to expand his limited perspective of what remote viewers could detect at a target site. Our fire drill experience helped me accept Hella's incident as having a synchronistic connection. I knew that Bob would not make a judgment on our fire drill encounter as synchronistic for him. He maintains high standards in his psi research and would not draw definite conclusions from a single event.

However, he acknowledged the irony of the incident. The Koestler Chair of Parapsychology would not exist were it not for Arthur Koestler's interest in synchronicity. Our experience may also have satisfied a subconscious need of his to observe a synchronicity.

"I believe that Arthur Koestler would have a lot to say about these fire drills and other examples of meaningful coincidences," Bob said. "I can understand why he thought that psi was at the roots of synchronicity."

I have often thought about the fire drill we came upon early that morning in Toronto. A cosmic trickster, synchronicity, had joined us and nudged our path toward a meaningful incident. I'm sure Arthur Koestler would have agreed.

18

A View Across

CAN SYNCHRONICITY BE BROUGHT ABOUT INTENTIONALLY AND PREDICTED? IF SO, I wondered, how does one know the difference between precognition and synchronicity? If the subsequent event fulfills a timely need, the incident appears to be synchronistic, even if it had been anticipated from psi impressions. Paths would be nudged to intersect when they would not have done so without the intent or the need.

If one were to dream of a specific letter coming in the mail and then it arrived the next day, that would be an alert, but it would not be synchronistic unless the unexpected letter contained timely information needed by the dreamer. The test is need and timing.

Sometimes we can sense approaching synchronistic events. We may wonder why we made a wrong turn in a familiar area or why we got off at the wrong subway stop. Why did we go into that store or talk to that stranger on an impulse? Has our path been gently nudged toward that meaningful intersection?

A few years ago, I was working on writing sections of a book, an early chapter of which, called "Mental Resonance," includes examples of precognition and synchronicity. As I reviewed my journal, I could find no clear recent incidents I could write about. I brooded over this lack of material and wondered if the highly synchronistic period of my life ten to fifteen years earlier had come and gone. Perhaps I had become too wrapped up in surface things or maybe daily demands were pulling me into too many routine activities. Possibly my creativity was being stifled as my work activities increased. What happened to those inspiring psi dreams? Could I rediscover my synchronistic connections?

By the time that weekend ended, a sense of longing had drifted out of shadows deep in my mind. I wanted to reexperience that sense of adventure, of awe, that precognitive or synchronistic experiences can evoke. My writing was blocked; the one-hundred-mile round-trip daily commute was grinding me down. It was time to go tracking again.

Two needs were clear: (1) that for new material for that chapter, and (2) a means to, once again, bring those deep currents to the surface.

During the next few days, my longing for an undefined something grew intense. I felt that it was time to call upon my precognitive, synchronistic, inner co-creators. My goal—my need—became clear: to seek a truly unique precognitive event to use for that chapter. I must reexperience that creative energy I knew I could access. My goal thus became one of synchronicity. The future incident would have meaning as material for my book and it would also provide the energizing needed for renewed creativity.

Then I upped the ante: I gave myself a limited time window. The event had to occur within the next week. I did not want to prolong this quest and daily activities were sure to force me back to the routine.

I had no travel plans, and this hoped-for synchronistic event would have to occur in my work environment or in the local area. Since my routine was well established, at least for several weeks, I initially felt that my hopes for a synchronistic experience within one week were unrealistic.

Those were tough requests. I hesitate to say demands, since I do not think we can ever demand a specific subconscious experience. We need to find that thin line between desire, intent, and demands. Demands keep our ego at centerstage too much; we run the risk of interfering with that subtle inner process. We send the wrong signal to our subconscious. As long as we keep a hopeful, respectful, cooperative attitude—similar to any creative collaboration—we can expect something to happen. It may not, but then we can shrug it off, move on, and try again later.

By the following Wednesday I had begun once again to feel those telltale tensions: a high degree of unrest and an acute sense of expectation. My exploring instinct was flying high. What was around the bend? What was hidden behind the ridge? Although I had several dreams that week, they clearly merely reflected my inner turmoil and routine events. Others were "thinking-in" dreams, a term I use for many dreamlike experiences with no dream imagery; I am asleep, conscious of thinking, but am simply in a "blackness," in which I review activities and invent scenarios.

By Friday, I still had experienced no unusual dream and a meaningful coincidence had yet to occur. I felt highly disappointed. I had hoped to have a new writing surge that weekend, which would have started with fresh dream material. That afternoon I paced around the yard and worked idly in the garage. In the evening I gazed at the Chesapeake Bay from our cliff. I could clearly see the small islands ten miles across near the Eastern Shore. The ospreys had returned. I watched them dive into the water for their daily catch. Immersed in that peaceful scene, I felt close to nature and became very relaxed, but the concern about having no material and not stirring up my creative energies was not far below that tranquil outer and inner landscape. My needs still flashed beneath a rippled surface.

Before falling asleep that night, I sent out my need, my call for help. I slept soundly. Late that night, I woke briefly, recalling no dream. I felt highly disappointed. Shortly before dawn, I awoke startled from an incredibly unusual dream:

I am driving somewhere and seem to get lost. I pull into a large parking lot, looking for a place to park. There is confusion in the lot; something is blocking my path. All around are huge tropical plants and I see a large crowd. I brush past the plants and move on. Ahead is a parking space and I pull in.

My attention is suddenly drawn to the car at my right. Something is odd about the driver. I look at him and am shocked to see him turn into a dog. Now a large dog is sitting in the driver's seat, paws on the wheel. The long-nosed dog glances at me; our eyes meet. I am puzzled, and wonder why it should be driving a car. Quickly, I back up and look for another spot.

Returning past the large plants, I find a space that has just been vacated. It is close to the store. I park and get out of the car. Then my car disappears and a large man is now lying on the ground where my car had been! He is naked from the waist up. As I watch, he grows heavier than he had been. I am puzzled.

Suddenly his body snaps into an incredible motion. He performs a strange exercise, moving only his upper body rapidly from horizontal to vertical. He snaps up and down, up and down. I notice his abdomen shake from the strain.

I woke up startled. The dream was extraordinarily vivid, almost lucid; the unusual dynamics very clear. Quickly I recorded the dream in detail. Images of the dog and the heavy man exercising invoked an uneasy feeling. This was one of the most bizarre dreams I had ever experienced.

Even though the dream was disturbing, I felt an intense creative surge when I awakened. I could make no sense of the dream and I couldn't reconcile that feeling of energized creativity with the troubling dream imagery.

Maybe my subconscious had overdramatized my own inner anxieties. I was in good physical shape and could not relate to any heavy man or the need to lose weight. I followed a good exercise regime—weightlifting, yard work, kayaking—and had no need for more. I could only record the details and wonder. At least I had something to write about and that sought-for energy had returned. Maybe that was the dream's only purpose.

My usual pattern on Saturday mornings included a short drive to Hay George's, a small deli three miles away, near Dares Beach, where I would buy coffee and the morning paper. After chatting with the locals, I would return home to begin weekend chores.

As I was driving there, I remembered an item needed for the garage. Though it was not important, I decided to go to the supermarket about five miles away. Then I would pick up coffee and the paper on my return. This was unusual, since I hardly ever passed by Hay George's in the morning without stopping for coffee.

When I pulled into the supermarket parking lot, I was surprised to see a large portion of the lot was roped off. Within that area was a large tent filled with tropical plants. A row of palmlike plants and tall ferns bordered the traffic lane. Even though it was early, the lot was nearly full. I turned into a lane at the tent, driving past taut ropes and overhanging branches. Memories of the dream that I had recorded a few hours earlier crept into consciousness. Something was beginning to trouble me.

At the far end of the lot, I saw a parking space. As I slowly pulled in to park, my attention was drawn to the car on my right. There it was: A large dog was sitting in the driver's seat!

There was my dream dog! As I gazed at the dog, a feeling of uneasiness swept over me. Irrationally, I pulled out of that parking spot and searched for another.

As I returned past the large tent, I noticed a sign announcing a special plant sale for that weekend. I was happy to see a vacancy that had not been there when I drove by earlier. I pulled in between a large van and a small car.

As I parked, I glanced around to be sure another dog was not sitting at the wheel. The car on my left was empty, but on my right a heavyset man was sitting at the wheel, gazing intently down at a newspaper.

I started walking toward the store through a small crowd of people who were milling around the plant tent. Something began to trouble me deeply. A sense of foreboding crept through me. I was reliving a dream and the events did not seem to be heading toward a pleasant ending. Quickly, I entered the store, and made my purchase.

As I left the store, I suddenly lost track of my surroundings. I seemed to be in another space, as though frozen in time. The environment I now occupied became surreal. Something seemed terribly wrong. Filled with a mixture of awe and anxiety, I puzzled at what I had stumbled into. Something was about to happen.

An elderly woman stood at a nearby phone booth. Her demeanor drew my attention. She seemed not to be present. Her gaze toward the parking lot was too vacant. Like myself, she seemed frozen in time. My eyes followed her stare, but I saw nothing unusual, only the plant tent.

I felt a profound sadness, possibly from the woman. Gradually a deep empathy crept through me. I felt very close to—somehow connected with—her. While we certainly shared something, I couldn't tell what. I quietly stood by wondering, and hoping that she was not ill.

Then I heard what I instantly knew was a clue for what was happening. At first the noise of the sirens was faint but soon the whine became ear-splitting. Before the ambulance turned, I knew that it was coming our way. It screeched around the corner, raced past us, and swerved into the row where I had parked jerking to a stop next to my car. Doors were flung open, paramedics leapt from the emergency vehicle, yanked open the door to the van, and jerked the heavy man to the ground.

I could not believe what I was seeing! The woman at the phone booth began to cry. Regaining composure, I ran to the paramedics and offered to move my car to give them more space. Upon finding another spot I returned to the emergency scene where I stood helplessly, watching, utterly amazed.

The paramedics threw a pad on the asphalt where my car had been, placed the man on it, and stripped off his shirt. He was now lying motionless on that pad, naked above the waist. One of the team pressed heavily on his chest, then released pressure, initiating CPR.

Press . . . Release . . . Press . . . Release.

The monitor connected to the man showed no vital signs. "Go to electricity!" shouted a paramedic. They placed paddles on his chest to jolt his heart back to life.

I had never seen anything like this before. The half-naked, unconscious man snapped up, then fell back every time the electric current surged into his body. He only moved from the waist up, like a hinged mannequin. The monitors only revealed bad news, a steady beep–beep–beep–beep.

The woman from the phone booth stood nearby, sobbing softly, not wanting to watch.

"We're not getting anywhere here! Let's run for it!" shouted a paramedic. They lifted the man into the emergency vehicle and raced away. Sirens grew fainter. In moments all was quiet. The onlookers drifted away. Someone helped the sobbing woman into the van and they slowly pulled ahead, turning in the direction the ambulance had gone.

At home I reviewed my journal to be sure my dream was as I remembered. Then I filled a few pages with new material. I regretted that I was unable to be of any direct assistance to the woman in the parking lot.

Maybe, at deep levels, I did reach out to her. I know that she had touched something deep within me. I had sensed her anguish, her fear of losing a loved one, her approaching grief.

This event led me to see that precognition and synchronicity are similar. Most of the time we have no clues that a synchronicity is emerging. However, our subconscious psi process has already made a prediction of an approaching meaningful event and has set in motion subconscious actions to help bring it about.

For me, this event fulfilled a need for a new precognitive experience. That, combined with the timing constraint, made this event synchronistic. There may have been another layer of synchronicities here. Several months later, a close friend died and I was better able to relate with the family in sharing their grief. Late that evening, I stood at the cliff, giving quiet thanks to my creative energies for allowing me to connect with that man and woman.

The incoming tide surged at the base of the cliff; tiny waves rippled into the distance. Across the bay, as dusk yielded to darkness, specks of yellow light clicked on one by one. I could now discern the boundary of the distant shore, the other side. I wondered about that man...to what distant shore had he gone? I realized that synchronicities can be strange and won-drous. They let us reach across time and space. They nudge us into mean-ingful intersections in times of need.

Developing Your
psi Potential

For me, the beauty of being psychic is in moving closer to
the wisdom of our own hearts. Though it can be simply a
means of information gathering, I've found its highest
value is in penetrating the layers of reality that reveal
the interconnectedness of all things.

➤ Judith Orloff, *Second Sight* (page 360)

We all have the potential to develop and use our natural psi ability. The keys lie in accepting the possibility of your psi nature, following a consistent approach when exercising that talent, and seeking ways to apply results. As with any talent, you learn by doing.

The following section examines the three types of ESP or psi experiences with which I have dealt in this book—remote viewing, psi dreams, and synchronicity. Remote viewing and psi dreams have much in common as they both emphasize visual imagery, although all other sensory modes can also come into play. Synchronicities are meaningful coincidences in response to pressing needs or concerns. The intuitive aspects of our psi nature nudge us into the right place at the right time. With intent and practice, we can frequently experience remote viewing, psi dreams, and synchronicities.

Initially you may want to pursue a simple approach to help you gradually link to your psi nature. By starting with a convenient and comfortable approach, you will easily initiate your psi processes. As you progress, it is important to refine your activities and adopt a systematic approach. These procedures are recommended to help you achieve results that can be easily evaluated and are free of possible biases. Of course, for spontaneous psi occurrences, keeping good records is invaluable for assessment of the experiences.

Through my own explorations and in working with others, I discovered that it does not matter what specific aspect of your psi nature you initially choose to explore. Developing proficiency in one makes it easier to experience others. Psi has many interwoven facets. You may choose to develop one of these facets more fully than the others, depending on your personal preferences, specific needs, and what is easiest for you at this time in your life. Anyone can achieve some level of psi proficiency, regardless of their environment or their cultural or ethnic background. Sometimes we have hunches, intuitions, psychic dreams, or seem to be lucky. These occurrences may have been triggered by psi impressions that simply had not surfaced into conscious awareness.

Experiencing remote viewing, tracking psi dreams, or seeking synchronicities will automatically enhance your subliminal and intuitive sensitivities.

Consider these psi practices as ways to develop your intuition. Similarly, if you have already explored intuition enhancement through meditation or simply by being alert to feelings and hunches, you will find it easier to do remote viewing, have psi dreams, or experience synchronicities.

On occasion, one form will be more appropriate than the others. For example, if you suddenly need to make an important decision, you may only have time to rely on intuition or gut feeling. If you need specific information, such as the location of something lost, remote viewing, a psi dream, or a synchronicity can be more helpful than intuition alone.

Intuition comprises two aspects. One results from a subconscious pattern-recognition type of logic that uses information from memory as well as all conventional senses, including the subliminal ones. The other aspect of intuition is primarily based on psi impressions that have not reached conscious awareness. The more we enhance our psi sensitivities, the better our intuition becomes.

Some people prefer to work within certain philosophical or metaphysical perspectives. As long as these pose no psychological constraints or do not invoke resistance, they can be extremely helpful. Choose whatever is positive and consistent with your intuitions.

People open to their psi talents are curious and adventuresome. They are willing to take a look and to suspend judgment. They are caring people who feel respect and concern for others. Children sometimes describe spontaneous psi experiences, including remote viewing impressions. Those who explore their inner nature can be seen as part of a cultural trend toward an integral, or holistic, society. They are not influenced or daunted by the difficulty others may have in considering the reality and practical benefits of the phenomena.

Since the natural ability is there within you, waiting in your subconscious, why not use it? We strive to improve our efficiency in many activities—athletics, the arts, professional skills—so it makes sense that we should strive to improve our native psi capabilities as well. They can help you sense surprise visitors or unexpected meetings, or locate something you or someone else have lost. As your psi proficiency improves, it can guide you to avoid dangerous or life-threatening situations. Psi talent can help you keep a step ahead of random acts of violence that frequently occur.

To begin your psi adventure, you need:

- ➤ motivation
- ➤ a willingness to accept the existence of the phenomena
- ➤ specific objectives
- ➤ strategies for goal setting, relaxing, and preparation
- ➤ approaches for initiating the psi process
- ➤ a dedicated journal for record keeping
- ➤ methods to evaluate and record results
- ➤ practice and perseverance.

Explore and discover which approach to psi development is most comfortable for you. It may be easier for you to set aside periods for relaxing than it is to recall dreams. Or you may prefer to seek psi in the dream state if you have trouble scheduling a consistent relaxation regime. You may prefer to rely more on synchronistic experiences or intuition than on seeking specific impressions.

As you uncover your natural psi talent, you will come to sense aspects of self that reach beyond your surface ego. You will feel a need to share your discoveries and seek ways for using your uncovered abilities to help others. You will sense a link with people and your environment and will be attracted toward activities that promote health, improve interpersonal effectiveness, and support humanitarian causes. These constructive endeavors will help you achieve a sense of purpose and well being.

Keep a balanced perspective and a sense of humor. Humor helps link us to our creative nature and to psi's domain.

19

Experiencing Remote Viewing

Something hidden. Go and find it...
Something lost behind the ranges...
Lost and waiting for you. Go!

—Rudyard Kipling, "The Explorers"

AS IN ANY SKILL DEVELOPMENT, YOU NEED MOTIVATION AND PATIENCE FOR DEVELOPING remote viewing proficiency. You can do remote viewing by yourself or with others. Working with companions is an exciting adventure in sharing.

Although remote viewing is primarily visual, other sensory experiences can occur. A remote viewer can sense feelings, motion, sounds, tastes, and aromas associated with the target. Sometimes a remote viewer simply knows or has thoughts about the unknown information but does not have sensory impressions.

Remote viewing occurs during a conscious but daydreamlike state of awareness. Many people report unexpected visual impressions that originate with remote viewing. In research laboratories, remote viewing has been demonstrated by people who do not suspect they have this capability.

Preliminaries

Sometimes unnecessary concerns keep us from trying to work with remote viewing, or they may slow our progress. Try to be aware of any resistance you may feel to describing a scene beyond your normal senses. If you do sense such resistance, ask yourself Why? Has someone in authority told you that remote viewing is impossible or nonsense? Are you afraid to be wrong? Are you bothered by the difficulty in understanding how it works? Are there other reasons?

When you have resolved these issues, you are ready to seek and reveal your remote viewing talent. You may prefer to work alone, at least initially, until you gain some degree of familiarity with the procedures and your remote viewing perceptions. If you choose to start on your own, however, you may eventually find that working with others is highly beneficial. It is much more fun. Working with others increases motivation and proficiency, and it also accelerates your learning process. A partner or partners can help you learn different methods of exploration and make your remote viewing activity more efficient. Like coaches, they can instill encouragement and self-confidence.

You can begin anytime. Simply accept the possibility that remote viewing phenomenon can occur and that you are capable and prepared to do it. Firm goal setting—simply affirming with conviction your intent to do remote viewing—an appropriate environment, a suitable level of relaxation, and practice are more important than any specific technique. The only equipment required is several sheets of plain paper and a pencil or a pen. The plain paper will not be distracting when you are sketching or writing impressions.

You do not need to be an expert artist. Simple sketches will do. It is a good idea to have colored pencils to show the hues you sense during your viewing sessions. If you prefer to describe your impressions verbally, use a voice-activated tape recorder or write your impressions on your notepaper.

Choosing a Target

Of course, you need a remote viewing goal—a target—something you want to sense or describe. You must not have any clues about the target or be able to anticipate what the specific target might be. Targets may be of any type: pictures, sketches, photographs, or objects, for example. Real locations are excellent remote viewing targets. Some people find it easier to describe real places than pictures or drawings of real places. For your initial remote viewing projects, it is best to use simple, easy-to-evaluate targets with only a few dominant elements. This will make it easier to confirm your impressions. As you gain confidence and proficiency, you can try more complex targets.

One way to do remote viewing alone is to choose a target location you have yet to see but can easily visit. After your session, travel there to check how well you did.

Another approach is to place a randomly selected, previously unseen playing card face down in front of you. Now remote view the color (red, black) or the suit (i.e., club, diamond, heart, or spade), of that card. It is best not to try number targets initially—even very experienced remote viewers have difficulty identifying them.

You may want to view something unique from your personal life coming your way within the next few days, or something specific that will be shown in the newspapers. Try to remote view your favorite cartoon or comic strip before looking at it in the morning paper.

A quick way of accessing target material is to insert a marker into an unopened magazine and then remote view only the page at that marker. Remember, however, that you may initially sense material printed on the page next to the intended one.

While you are a passenger, try to remote view an approaching scene that is some distance ahead. Try to describe the appearance of someone you do not know—before you meet them. What is coming to you in the mail? Mark Twain frequently foresaw unexpected details of letters that he received the next day.

Have a colleague select and observe a target—a picture, a location, or an object—during your remote viewing session. Pictures from *National Geographic* or similar pictorial magazines are excellent targets. Then compare your impressions with the actual target.

Preparation

Certain activities can help the remote viewing process, including artistic pursuits and visualization exercises.

The left hemisphere of the brain is usually the dominant area for logical, linear, sequential, and analytical thought, including language and the sense of time. The right hemisphere is associated with functions that are nonlinear, such as pattern recognition and artistic talents. Remote viewing impressions are more reliable when they are sketches or other nonanalytical forms than when they are analytical or specific names. This suggests that our right-brain hemisphere has a primary role in the processing of remote viewing impressions. Thus, any activity that improves our artistic abilities enables us to be more receptive and better able to process remote viewing data. By actively pursuing painting or music or developing some other art form, we automatically exercise that region of the brain that most closely links with the remote viewing process. Drawing or sketching with your left hand, especially if you are right-handed, is another good practice for exercising right-hemisphere activity.

Improving visualization ability can be a valuable tool for the remote viewing process. When we begin to explore remote viewing, our impressions very likely will be faint and fleeting images. Visualization exercises enhance our ability to hold onto fleeting remote viewing impressions and to recognize them better.

Some people prefer to set aside frequent relaxation or meditation periods for achieving inner awareness. These practices are extremely helpful for sensitizing us to remote viewing impressions. Procedures for developing intuition are also beneficial.

Stimulating both the left- and right-brain hemispheres improves coherence of brain-hemisphere activity. This can help in the remote viewing process, since the emerging impressions can be better integrated. Music is one means of stimulating both hemispheres and it also can help with brain-hemisphere synchronization. Some prefer low, soothing rhythms; others relate better to dynamic sounds. Perhaps music characterized by repeated tones or specific frequencies will be helpful or you may prefer nonrepeating sounds, like ocean surf.

Some people prefer to improve left/right brain–hemisphere coherence by using biofeedback equipment. These devices monitor electrical activity in the brain by means of sensors placed on the scalp. Lights on the display monitor indicate how well brain-hemisphere electrical activity—brain waves—are synchronized and in balance. With practice, both hemispheres can be brought into balance through mental intention alone.

You can practice visualization by relaxing and imagining a scene or object. How vivid is the image? How long can you "see" it? Is it like a daydream or more lasting? Visualization exercises will make it easier to retain and recognize remote viewing images, which at first may be faint and brief.

It can be helpful to walk in a park or along a city street imagining that you are experiencing remote viewing impressions. Carefully observe and touch various objects. Listen to the sounds, notice the aromas. Remind yourself that later on you will want to experience something similar during a remote viewing session. This not only helps sharpen all your senses and subliminal perceptions, it also improves your intuitive sensitivities.

Any activity that improves physical and psychological balance is helpful for inner exploration and improving remote viewing proficiency. The level of exercise does not need to be intense. Mild activity, such as slow walking, or whatever is comfortable can be sufficient. These activities give you an opportunity to keep focus on your intent to do remote viewing. The more regularly you keep your intent in mind, the more likely your goals can be achieved.

When you feel ready, find a comfortable place that is relatively free of distraction such as the telephone, TV, unexpected visits, or sudden noise. Call this place your "sanctuary." At first, your level of relaxation may vary from a calm, receptive state to deep meditation, but eventually you will be able to practice remote viewing while only in a daydreamlike state. Whatever your level of internal awareness, you always remain conscious and have control. The period of time when you are relaxed and receptive to remote viewing impressions is called the remote viewing session. As you approach your session, frequently affirm your desire to view the intended target. You may wish to write out your objective; this can help reinforce your remote viewing intent and be treated as a request for subconscious assistance.

When you are ready to begin remote viewing from your sanctuary, sit comfortably in a chair and place both feet on the floor. The lighting should be low to minimize any distractions that may be present in the room. You do not need to close your eyes, although you may prefer to do so.

Reaffirm your desire for doing remote viewing. Mentally repeat: "In a few minutes, I will be ready to remote view the target." You may prefer to give the target a label, such as "T–1." If so, think: "I am preparing to remote view T–1." You may do this several times. Focusing thought on this intent activates the inner processes that lead to remote viewing perceptions. You may prefer to vocalize your intent for increased emphasis.

After mentally or verbally repeating your goal intent several times, begin a cool-down phase, during which you minimize your usual thinking patterns. The remote viewing process is easily blocked by routine thoughts and ordinary sensory activity. Try a variety of cool-down strategies to find out what works best for you. Focusing on breathing, or following a progressive relaxation technique are just two of the numerous methods. For example, follow this simple breathing technique: Gradually take a deep breath, hold it for three or four seconds, then slowly breathe out. Pause for three or four seconds, then repeat this cycle. Keep all your attention on your breathing.

You may modify this procedure by imagining a countdown from ten to one during which you make mental, self-directed suggestions for achieving a calm state by the time you reach the count of one. Count down every time you breath out. With each out-breath think, "I am becoming more and more relaxed."

A variety of approaches can be used to achieve a calm, relaxed state. Many of them use imagery that has a peaceful association and invokes a calming feeling. Transition from normal awareness to detachment and calmness can be achieved by guided imagery that gradually progresses to scenes symbolic of deep, unconscious levels, which have a naturally calming effect. For example, imagining descending stairs to an ancient doorway can bring about strong feelings of detachment and an openness to whatever may be at yet-deeper levels. Guided imagery can move us naturally into a calming scene, such as walking along a path into a beautiful garden or quiet forest. Another effective method for achieving a calming state is to recall memories of a time when you experienced an intense feeling of peace, such as a moonlight walk along a mirror-smooth lake, visiting a memorial garden, or attending a mountain retreat. Maybe you experienced calm feelings during a special shared moment with someone. Reliving experiences like these brings back the peace and calm you once experienced and helps you achieve a relaxed state again.

Some people can achieve calmness by focusing on nonspecific imagery, such as being bathed in a gentle, white light that invokes a warm and comfortable feeling. Sometimes imagining feelings of floating or weightlessness, perhaps from swimming or underwater diving, can help recreate a relaxed state. Experiment to discover what approach is best for you. With practice, reaching a calm state can be very natural and easier to achieve.

When you feel relaxed and ready to receive inner impressions, turn off the music, if any, or keep it very low to help mask background noise. Acknowledge your desire to be a partner, a co-creator, with your subconscious mind. Be curious…be expectant…anticipate a gift…look forward to your remote viewing present. You are now ready to explore your remote viewing talent.

Initiating the Process

Begin the remote viewing process by thinking with confidence: "I am now ready to remote view the target." Try several versions of this statement to discover the wording best for you. Try "I am ready to access the target." After this statement of preparation, shift focus to your intent or desire, such as "I desire to access the target." You can shorten this to "access the target." Or phrase your intent in terms of a question. "What is the target?" Later, these objective statements can be shortened simply to "Access," or "What?" If a colleague is observing the target, you can think: What is the target my colleague is observing? If you have given the target a label, you can think Access T–1. "As long as you state the intent and specific objectives carefully before you begin, the shorthand—*Access*, or *What?*—will suffice and won't be distracting. Thinking Access frequently during your period of relaxation reaffirms your remote viewing intent. It keeps your conscious mind focused and minimizes internal noise and chatter. You may experience cycles of relaxation that are deep at times and close to normal consciousness at others. Whenever you approach normal consciousness, simply repeat: "Access," or "What?" and wait for impressions. Some people find that generating a sense of connectivity, or unity, with the target assists the remote viewing process.

Initially, some people like to have a session helper who's only purpose is to help you keep focused on the objective. *This helper must have no knowledge of the target.* If you start remote viewing with a session helper, have him or her sit quietly in front of you. When you are ready, your helper will softly repeat the objective—"You are ready to view the target"; "You can now access the target"; "What is T–1?" etc. These requests can also be shortened—"Access the target"; "Access"; "What?"; or simply "Target"—and occasionally repeated.

Wait for whatever impressions come to you. You may imagine a blank screen and anticipate remote viewing images appearing on that screen. Visualize entering an inner sanctuary that has a room with a view of your target. Move toward that window and look at the target. Try various strategies. Whatever strategy you choose, anticipate sensing the target whenever you repeat or hear "Access," "What?" or "Target." Wait patiently and expectantly for impressions of the desired target.

The Session

In a few moments, fleeting images and impressions will appear. Welcome them. Pay attention to them. Some may be fragments and others may be complete forms. Take note of the impressions' shapes and colors. Do you feel any sensation or have any sense of activity? Do any thoughts pop into your mind? Sketch or briefly write your initial perceptions, no matter how vague.

Continue with this cycle of affirmation and expectant waiting. Note all impressions. Occasionally, your session helper may ask for clarification of what you have sketched. If you are alone, occasionally review your emerging sketches and pose a request: "I desire more detail," or ask: "Is there anything else at this target?" Simply sketch or describe your perceptions— do not analyze them or try to name them. Interpreting them at this stage can break the subconscious flow and block new impressions that are about to emerge. This can also add noise and distort the basic image.

At first, you may want to be open to any perception of whatever is at the target. This approach will help you determine your natural preferences. For example, you may first naturally pick up on colors, then shapes or forms later in the session. Or you may proceed in a systematic way by focusing intent on perceiving only certain types of impressions in a specific order. For example, you may desire to perceive only dominant configurations or shapes, then progress through color, feelings, motions, or other sensory impressions. Or you may devote one session to seeking general impressions and a later session to refinement of the initial impressions.

Another strategy is to focus on specific types of information and not other aspects of the target. For example, you could remote view dominant colors and configurations, but not any other target aspect. Or perhaps your focus would be only on detecting activity at the target. If you find that you are not particularly good at visualizing, you may prefer to seek feelings, sounds, sensations, smells, or other nonvisual, sensory impressions about the target. You may even have thoughts about the target but no sensory impressions. That is fine. We all have different cognitive styles and preferences. Only through experiment will you discover your own.

Some remote viewers prefer to develop impressions of the target from their kinesthetic responses. This means they simply sketch whatever they feel is at the target. They may not have any visual impressions. Instead they allow the drawing to develop by itself, much as an artist might do when creating new forms. By relaxing, detaching from analytical thinking, and allowing the drawing to create itself, the remote viewer can produce an accurate representation of the target. The viewer allows the target to be expressed by responding to an impulse to draw what is felt to be at the target. At first, the process may feel like random doodling. With practice, the rough sketches become more like drawings. This kinesthetic way of capturing target impressions can also be achieved by working with modeling clay and forming a three-dimensional representation of the target.

Kinesthetic response is similar to the process where a remote viewer simply has thoughts about the target, even though no visual or other sensory impressions are received. Sometimes, both thoughts and kinesthetic impressions occur.

Typically a remote viewing session lasts thirty minutes, but it may be shorter or longer, depending on your level of proficiency and the nature of the viewing objective. Your remote viewing session is over when impressions or responses cease, or when you begin to feel restless and naturally return to alert, conscious awareness. If you reached a deep state of relaxation, you should gradually resume normal activity. Review all the impressions that came to you during the session, and then write a brief summary. The act of writing demonstrates a strong interest in remote viewing that enhances the remote viewing process.

After Remote Viewing

When finished with your review, you may want to analyze or interpret your impressions. First underline in your summary the impressions that you felt to be strongest. Maybe a color seemed dominant; maybe it was a certain feeling. Perhaps one image seemed more clear than the others. Then take a look at all the impressions to see if you can detect a pattern or theme. Was there a predominance of vertical lines in your images? Did you feel a sensation of rising? Maybe the target depicts thin, tall shapes pointing sky-ward. Did you glimpse a humanlike shape—possibly a person at a scene or a picture of someone?

If you are working with a beacon person who is at a real site, see if your impressions have locational clues. Did you glimpse a lake and the only one nearby is in the city park? Perhaps your friend was on a roller coaster and you felt a sinking feeling during the session. Your impressions may have resembled Polynesian themes or you thought of Hawaiian music and your friend was at a Polynesian restaurant. Whatever your impressions are, examine their overall patterns for identifying the general nature of the tar-get. Then see if you can narrow down target possibilities. Write down the general and specific interpretations based on your impressions.

Now you are ready to learn the identity of the target. This is akin to opening your psi gift and you should enjoy it to its fullest: Sense the antici-pation of opening your remote viewing present. Expect it to match your perceptions. Then go see—and be pleasantly surprised. Observing the tar-get as soon as possible after each session is known as receiving feedback or ground truth. As in any learning-related task, we need feedback to rein-force the developing process.

Did you sense any overall features, such as vertical or horizontal lines, or their general orientation? You may have detected colors, or felt a sense of motion associated with the target. Those motions may relate to activity present or implied at a location, or suggested by dominant geometries. For example, a waterfall may have invoked a feeling of falling. If the target was a picture of a snow-covered mountain, you may have felt a cold sensation even if you did not have any images of snow or ice. In the beginning, you may find your remote viewing perceptions are only approximate with a mix of correct and incorrect elements. Refinement comes with practice.

As you compare your impressions to the actual target, look for your natural preferences. You may generally do well describing dominant colors or sensations associated with the target and not as well when trying to identify other aspects of the target. You may prefer colors or feelings. You may be attracted to architecture or prefer perceiving natural or human elements to those that are artificial. Were your initial images or nonvisual impressions more accurate than later ones? You find out through practice, evaluation, and more practice.

In order to keep track of your progress, you may want to use a simple recording procedure. For example, you could assign an *H* when your impressions have a high correlation to the target; an *M* when about half the impressions are correct; and an *L* when there are only a few correlations. If you start out with a series of *L*s, don't be discouraged. Simply stick with it and you will improve. As you work with a variety of target types, you may discover patterns and preferences. You may do well on some types of targets and not on others, as least initially.

Remember, your impressions will have better correlation with shapes, configurations, colors, feelings, or other nonanalytical features of the target. Specific interpretive aspects of the target—names, functions, or meanings we give it—will probably remain elusive. With practice, however, it will become easier to identify generic target classes. A tall mountain is perceived as a mountain and not a ridge. A city is perceived as a city, not a village, but a city without a specific name. In some cases, a single remote viewing image can provide a clue for identifying a specific place. For example, you may perceive a city area near a large river, but are not sure what city it is unless you also perceive a large arch which could suggest that the target site is St. Louis. With focus on perceiving specifics, it is possible to improve remote viewing perceptions to include the specific names of the targets.

It is important to keep good records. Begin and maintain a journal of your impressions from each session that you will keep along with a photo, sketch, or other information about the target. Monitor your progress and note factors that may have affected results. Are some times better than others? If so, why do you think this was the case? Were certain types of targets easier to sense than others? Were there any correlations with mood, fatigue, or daily concerns that may have influenced results? As you gain experience, you can develop comprehensive ways of assessing your impressions. Like any acquired skill, remote viewing requires feedback and diligent evaluation.

After your session, you may also want to perform simple physical activity to help you maintain good physical and mental well-being. Overemphasis on any inner activity, whether artistic or analytical, can be taken to extremes. The key to inner exploration is balance. Adequate rest and diet and maintenance of moderation in all activities and aspects of our lives improves the efficiency of our psi explorations.

As You Progress

After several sessions, you should find that remote viewing has become easier. You may want to continue by developing a systematic approach for proficiency and for exploring specific applications. If you started remote viewing alone, ask others to join you in this adventure. Such a partner can help you prepare and select targets or be a session helper or a beacon person who observes or visits the target during a session. Taking turns practicing the various roles is a great way to enhance learning for everyone.

An important element of remote viewing is continuing to practice with a variety of targets. You may want to expand some of the approaches discussed previously, such as describing details on a specific magazine page or exploring events that are about to take place. Remote view a target that will be selected after your session. This method also calls into play precognition.

Ask a friend to imagine a target for you, which he or she may choose to sketch. When you remote view the target, you may be accessing the sketch or the image of the target held in your friend's thoughts.

Another way to expand on remote viewing activity is to have a colleague choose a variety of targets, seal them in opaque envelopes, and place them in a target pool. This pool can contain several dozen targets, depending on your remote viewing pace. For example, if you are working with pictures, your colleague can select a dozen diverse pictures that have dramatic elements with easy-to-identify shapes and distinct boundaries. They can have vivid colors or invoke feelings or actions. Postcards, art prints, slides, or pictures taken from magazines can be used. Your colleague can randomly choose one of those targets, and open and observe it as a beacon person during your remote viewing session. Should you want to work without a beacon person, have your colleague randomly select a target and keep it unopened during your session. If your colleague gives the target pool to you, then you need to randomly select one of the sealed envelopes, making sure there is no way you can know any of the contents of the target envelope.

The targets need to be diverse and easily distinguishable. If some overlapping features occur, they should differ from one another in some way—color, perspective, or size, for example. Be sure the opposite side of picture targets are blank, otherwise they may become confused with the remote viewing target.

You could also have a colleague prepare several types of target pools by which you can explore your preferences. For example, one target pool can be mainly natural scenes and architectural features; while another has pictures of animals or plants. If you want to work with three-dimensional objects, have a colleague assemble a variety of small items and place them inside film cans. You can randomly select one of the cans at your leisure and remote view the contents.

Real locations are great targets. Such a target pool will contain names of places written on cards, each of which is placed in a separate envelope. Each site must have features that make it distinct from all the other target sites. The sites can be visited easily or they may be anywhere on Earth. As you improve, see if you can identify the specific location based on your remote viewing impressions. This type of target pool builds proficiency for locating missing people or objects.

As you progress, develop target pools for specific interests and talents. For example, you may want to explore the medical-diagnostics potential of remote viewing. Have a colleague prepare names compiled from consenting individuals with specific medical conditions and place their names in separate envelopes. Then choose one of the envelopes at random and, without opening it, remote view the medical condition of the individual identified inside that envelope. After your impressions are recorded for each target envelope, your colleague can check to see which names were inside each envelope, then compare your results to the known medical data for those individuals.

A carefully prepared target pool makes it easier to initiate a remote viewing session at any time. A number of groups and organizations, which you may wish to contact, have already developed target pools. Several options are now available on the Internet and more are soon to evolve (see page 209).

Many possibilities exist for target-pool development. The more diversity in your target pool, the more you can learn about your remote viewing talent. Whatever target your colleague has prepared, you can choose to work alone with it or have someone keep it for you. If you choose to work alone, simply choose a target envelope at random and place it nearby or in another room. Random selection assures that you can only remote view that target and not be influenced or otherwise affected by someone else's expectation. Random selection also keeps focus on the idea of target unpredictability and eliminates guessing tendencies that block or distort emerging remote viewing impressions. Knowing that the target is unpredictable minimizes our natural inclinations for premature interpretation of emerging impressions.

It sometimes helps to assign each target an arbitrary address or label, such as Envelope E–1, or Remote Location L–2. This label can have a role in helping your subconscious psi process find the target. Arbitrary labels or target designators also help in record keeping.

If someone else keeps your target pool, that person can randomly select and label the target. You have the option of remote viewing the target specified or identified in the envelope, or you can have your colleague open the envelope and serve as a beacon person. Some people find it helpful to have someone look at the target or object, or visit the target site if the target pool consists of physical locations. While the beacon person may play a role in helping you find the target, it is not necessary to focus on the beacon person's knowledge of that target. Remote viewing can operate independently of someone else's thoughts. The beacon person can be in the same building, or across the country. He or she then observes or visits the target during your remote viewing session and they may also photograph or sketch it at that time.

Following the remote viewing session, the beacon person returns from the place where he or she observed the target. Once you have finished summarizing your impressions, the beacon person will show you the picture or object or take you to the site for ground-truth feedback. If the beacon person is at a distant location, he or she can provide feedback by phone and follow up with a picture or photo by mail or fax.

The beacon person will inform you of anything that may have occurred but may not be obvious, such as sudden distractions or unusual action. You may have sensed them, too, and those impressions are valuable as well as great learning experiences.

After you have gained some experience ask a friend who is traveling to be a beacon person. At prearranged times, remote view his or her environment or activities. You will both be pleasantly surprised to see how well you did—it's as though you had been along on the journey.

One of the best ways to track your progress is to have someone present four possible targets to you, one of which is the actual target. You then try to select the correct target based only on your remote viewing perceptions. The four possible targets should be as diverse as possible to minimize chances that one of the perceptions appears on some or all the other targets. The targets can be pictures, photos, objects, or real sites that you can visit. This method allows for statistical evaluation, since chance on average would result in one correct guess in every four attempts. If for every four remote viewing sessions you are able to select the correct target three times, you are on your way to high proficiency.

The variety of possible projects and target pools demonstrates just how diverse remote viewing can be, and it also points out the degree of your connectivity to others and the environment.

Applying Remote Viewing

You may be satisfied simply knowing that we are all interconnected in some way. That knowledge alone is valuable. It shows that our current understanding of the physical universe is incomplete and that we are deeply connected with one another and with our environment. Our thoughts and intentions are not isolated events, but can reach out to others even when we are unaware they are doing so. However, as you develop proficiency, you may want—or need—to apply your new skills.

You may have opportunities to use your skills for locating something you or someone else have lost—a ring, for example. Are any of your loved ones or friends ill, or even in danger? You may want to remote view the future to detect anything coming your way that may call for preparation or even avoidance. There are a variety of practical roles for remote viewing talent.

As you continue experiencing remote viewing, your subliminal sensitivities become sharper. You will notice an increase of synchronicities in your life. You will become more intuitive. You may feel "luckier." Psychic dreams will increase.

Since remote viewing and creativity are closely related, the pursuit of remote viewing proficiency may help in a variety of creative endeavors. You will gain insight and life for new projects such as writing, music, dance, designing, or communication. You may discover buried talents. Your increased sensitivity will help you relate to the situations of others and improve your interpersonal skills. Remote viewing touches deep layers in our psyche and can stir up healing energies that enhance our sense of well-being and state of health.

Explore to see how remote viewing works best for you. Let your spirit of adventure and imagination be your guide.

20
Tracking psi Dreams

The psyche...possesses a latent ESP capacity that is most
likely to be deployed during sleep, in the dreaming phase.
Psi is no longer the exclusive gift of rare beings known as
psychic sensitives, but is a normal part of human existence, capable of being experienced by nearly everyone
under the right conditions.

—Ullman, Krippner, and Vaughan, *Dream Telepathy* (page 227)

WE HAVE AN INNATE CURIOSITY ABOUT THE FUTURE—WHAT WILL HAPPEN TO US OR
our loved ones in the next few days? What unexpected incident is
approaching? Psi researchers suspect that our natural psi abilities are active
at a subconscious level most of the time and that through some type of psi
scanning or searching mode, we reach out to discover what we need to
know. Every night we have from six to eight dreams, even though we may
recall only a few or none of them. Our dream state can be a rich source of
personal insight. Dreams can also provide information of an extrasensory
or psi nature that can help us in many ways. The most common, easiest
way to explore the nature of psi is by means of our dreams. Reports of psi
dreams are found going back thousands of years, from all cultures.

Psi dreams can be personal or impersonal. They can occur spontaneously or be sought intentionally. As in any ESP or remote viewing activity, they can also be examined systematically. Through psi dreams, we can
directly experience what is sensed intuitively. In the dream, you may be an
observer of the action or a participant. In some instances, you may
become lucid, or consciously aware that you are dreaming. As you continue working with your dreams, it is not uncommon to experience them in a
lucid form. In a lucid dream, we are active participants in the dream drama.

We can alter unpleasant situations, understand their causes, and gain confidence for confronting similar issues in our daily life. Lucid dreams give us an opportunity to explore new activities. Some individuals improve skills by practicing them while lucid dreaming. Creating a new self-image of well-being or health in a lucid dream is helpful in recovery from a serious illness or injury.

As in any dream, a psi dream may present us with impressions representing all our senses and sensitivities—sight, sound, touch, smell, feelings, and motion. Dreams are a dynamic way to experience our natural psi talent directly. It is likely that we all have psi dreams, but do not recall them. For example, when we awaken we may have a hunch, a feeling, or an intuition that resulted from a psi dream we do not recall.

Usually, we experience psi dreams when we have a need to do so. They may alert us to a current situation or to someone else's intentions. Similar to remote viewing, they may show us the location of something we have lost or someone who is missing. Many psi dreams contain information that helps us respond to approaching news or an emerging event, or they provide details for a current activity or need. Most psi dreams occur spontaneously. However, most any time we desire to do so, we can experience psi dreams as a natural part of our nightly dreamscape. All that is required is motivation and intent.

Some people may feel that opening up the psi-dream gate is like opening a floodgate. They fear a loss of control; they dread being deluged with information they do not want or will not know how to handle. However, there is no evidence to suggest our psi dreams will swamp us. We all have some type of subconscious filter that regulates what we experience or recall in any dream. As in any psi pursuit, you are in control. You can turn off psi experiences whenever you want to by communicating to your unconscious that you do not want to have them.

People sometimes report having strong emotional responses to psi dreams. Such reactions can be minimized with practice and the intention of experiencing only what is necessary for understanding the dream message. Dreams often overdramatize the nature of the event in order to get our attention and to help us with recall.

Some people have concerns about working with any form of psi perception. They fear that it may make it possible to access private or personal information about themselves or others, but this should not be a concern. Our psi facilities are subconscious and any truly private information is filtered or blocked by our, or the other person's, subconscious psi and dream filters. In certain cases, however, such filters may be relaxed when an awareness of the information is beneficial for self and others and fulfills a constructive goal. For example, it is possible to have a psi dream that helps to solve a crime, even though the criminal wants to remain unknown.

We can all begin an exciting journey of discovery through which we uncover the natural extrasensory or psi talent that is available while we are asleep and dreaming.

Preparation

You can begin to explore your psi dream potential at any time. As with remote viewing, the primary requirement is the desire—the intention—to have them.

There are, however, issues that may affect your progress. Certain overindulgences can impede ordinary dreaming. Research has shown that some people are sensitive to alcohol and certain drugs to the extent that these substances block dreaming and dream recall or distort dream content. Barbiturates are neurological suppressants that block our natural rapid-eye movement (REM) dream cycle. Individuals who are habitual users of such substances have reduced REM-dream periods. Prescription drugs are not evaluated for their impact on our dreaming cycle and it is difficult to know which ones have more dream-suppressing effect than others. Illegal nonprescription drugs, while reported to generate intense mental imagery, including lucid dreams, have not been found to be helpful for psi experiences. Psi impressions, should they occur, are likely to be distorted and extremely difficult to interpret. Some psychological states may also interfere, especially if conditioned by fear, biases, or resentments.

State of mind prior to sleep has a significant effect on dream content and our dreams will very likely reflect our moods and concerns. Even if a psi dream should occur, it will probably be diffused by dream elements that are dominated by our worries or fears. While psi dreams can occur at any time for anyone, they are easier to experience and understand if our life is in good physical and mental balance. Maintaining good health and pursuing activities that promote psychological well-being minimize internal disturbances that can adversely affect our subconscious psi process. With a balanced lifestyle and an open, caring attitude toward others, you can expect to experience psi dreams.

As with any dreamwork, all you need is a notepad and a pen or pencil within easy reach from your bed. After each dream, simply record key impressions on this notepad. Later, when you have fully awakened, transfer your notes along with all the details you can recall into your dedicated dream journal. Some people prefer to verbally describe their dreams to a voice-activated tape recorder; however, this is not necessary and can be distracting to others.

Initiating psi Dreams

A place to sleep undisturbed and some strategies are all that is required to initiate the psi-dream process.

First, begin a practice of recalling as many dreams as possible each night. Simply intend to have them. A sincere desire to remember them will eventually open your dream gate. Become used to recalling your dreams, no matter what they are. Reading about dreams will illustrate their viability and give you confidence that you can also recall them.

Although you may occasionally have spontaneous psi dreams, you need an objective if you want to experience them more frequently. Your initial psi-dream objective can be for any current need, such as providing insight into a pending job interview or offer or concerning a personal-relationship situation. Eventually, your objectives may become less personal. For example, you may intend to dream of an approaching incident that will be reported in a newspaper. Or perhaps you will intend to dream about anything of interest coming your way in the near future. You can also borrow a technique from remote viewing and insert a marker into a magazine you have never opened and intend to dream the content of the marked page. A place you have not yet seen but can easily visit is another good psi-dream objective. If someone requests your help with a personal issue and its possible cause, perhaps a buried memory from childhood, a psi dream can provide insight for discussion.

You may want to explore psi dreams in a systematic way. Ask a colleague to select a target for you to dream about. This could be an art print, a photo, a real place, an object, or almost anything. It is not necessary for your colleague to observe this target while you are dreaming. It may have been selected earlier or may be chosen in the immediate future. Activities such as these provide excellent practice for improving psi-dream proficiency.

When you decide that you are ready to explore psi dreams, frequently repeat your psi-dream objective during the day. If you desire to dream of a scene unknown to you, you may want to walk in a garden or park and imagine that you are actually experiencing a psi dream. Observe your environment closely; touch and feel a tree, a rock, a building. Carefully observe anything present—structures, natural features, people, animals, plants. Remind yourself that, later on, you will be visiting an unknown target in a dream. Walking around and being observant while thinking about your dream intent helps energize your subconscious psi process. You may want to sketch the scene, imagining that you are drawing a dream scene. This helps reinforce your desire to experience a psi dream and remember its details.

Later, as you prepare for sleep, reaffirm you psi-dream objective. Simply state: "Tonight, I desire to have any psi dream," or "Tonight, I desire to have a psi dream to help with—." If you desire a psi dream to provide information on a specific target, you can say: "Tonight, I desire to dream about target—." Your request can be general or very specific. For example, if you are seeking a new house or apartment, your request could be: "I desire a psi dream to help me in my search for a new place to live," or "I desire a psi dream with enough details to indicate the place best-suited for me to live." As you drift off to sleep, repeat your intent several times. Write out your objective and place it next to your notepad or under your pillow. In other words, sleep on it!

When you wake up, if you recall no dream, simply reaffirm your psi-dream intent as you drift back to sleep. Keep reaffirming your intent throughout the night if necessary.

Recalling psi Dreams

Initially, you may have difficulty remembering dreams, even though you know you did dream. The key to dream recall is intent. By lying perfectly still for several minutes and repeating the desire to recall that dream, it will slowly emerge. The stronger you set your desire to recall dreams, including psi dreams, the easier it will be to remember them when you wake up. As you gain experience recalling any dream, it will become easier to recall psi dreams.

At first, you may only remember a dream when you wake up. It may have been the last dream you had during sleep, or it may have been one that occurred earlier. It is best to wake up immediately after each dream and jot down keywords at that time, while the dream is still fresh. You don't need to write out all the details. Keywords will prompt easy dream recall later. Force yourself to write a keyword or two, if necessary. That act reinforces your intent and improves subsequent dream recall and note-making ability. Fixing an intent to wake up after each dream before you drift back to sleep will eventually lead to timely dream recall. Even if you do not succeed at first, persistence will eventually open your dream gate. Once your dream gate is opened, you will recall a variety of dreams naturally. If you want to work with them, though they may not be psi dreams, they can give you insight into day-to-day issues and concerns. Both types, personal and psi dreams, can greatly assist with daily activities and your journey of self-discovery.

You may prefer to begin dreamwork by focusing your intent to recall only your last dream. Your last dream cycle occurs at or near the time you wake up naturally and will be easier to recall than any of the earlier dreams. By keeping focus on recalling only one dream—the last one—you are signaling its importance to your subconscious and the most significant dream will very likely occur around the time you wake up and not earlier. The last dream often appears as a summary of earlier ones. Focusing on recalling only one dream is a simpler way to begin dreamwork than by being open to recalling some or all of the six or eight dreams that occurred. As you gain proficiency in recalling that last dream, you may automatically recall others, even if you did not wake up after each one. However, if you do not recall other dreams and want to explore them, simply refocus your intent to recall them. This will lead to waking up after other dreams and to their recall.

You may discover impressions of the target can occur in that transition state as you are just waking up. Similarly you may have target impressions just as you drift off to sleep. Perceptions in these phases are often like remote viewing perceptions.

As we explore dream recall, we may discover that some times are better than others. Normal cycles in our body chemistry, our biorhythms, and external factors may affect our dream cycles and their content. A recent psi data–research review indicates that psi effects are stronger around certain sidereal times—those measured relative to the solar system—and not the twenty-four-hour Earth rotation.

A helpful psi dream–recall strategy is to set aside a certain night when you expect to be relaxed and designate that to be your night for remembering psi dreams. As you gain experience, you will remember psi dreams more frequently and more easily. However, you may not experience psi dreams whenever you desire them. As with any creative activity, do not become discouraged. Keep at it. With practice, psi-dream recall will eventually occur. Psi dreams usually account for only a small portion of our total dream inventory, but, depending on intent and need, they can occur frequently.

Identifying psi Dreams

Identifying psi dreams becomes easier once we gain experience with ordinary dreams. The development of various strategies—such as seeking psi dreams on certain nights, or relying on certain symbols or feelings—helps identify them.

Our usual dreams can have a wide range of content. Some express our hopes and desires; others may rehash daily events or rehearse future plans. Still others may reveal hidden concerns or fears that we need to resolve. Ordinary dreams may be literal, symbolic, or a mixture of both.

Many approaches exist for working with ordinary dreams and for integrating their insights into daily life. The list of selected readings at the end of this book includes references to books that are useful in pursuing personal dreamwork.

A good strategy for interpreting any dream is to explore it from a psychological level first. What does this dream represent about me, an aspect of me, or a concern of mine? For example, a dream about a friend could illustrate a quality that the individual embodies, which I have or lack. If a psychological interpretation does not seem relevant, move on to explore the psi aspects of the dream.

As with ordinary dreams, psi dreams can be literal or symbolic. In literal psi dreams, the dream elements generally depict what they represent. For example, a remote scene can be reconstructed in great detail; a painting used as a target can be seen exactly as that painting actually appears. If you dream of a friend you haven't seen for a long time, it is likely that he or she desires to communicate. Perhaps you will receive a letter or a call shortly. If you want your dreams to be as realistic as possible, simply include that intent with your presleep objectives.

Symbolic psi dreams usually alert us to a general future possibility, but do not reveal the specifics. Symbolic dreams may occur partially to shield us from something we are not ready to accept. For example, if a loved one has been injured in an accident, our psi dream may translate that information into an accident involving someone else whom we know—or an unrecognized person—whose predicament would not be as uncomfortable for us. The basic message comes through, but the details do not.

A dream that we suspect to be of psi origin, but which appears to be a combination of the literal and the symbolic, may be difficult to understand. Maybe the symbolism was too general or the imagery incomplete or ambiguous. Focusing on having a follow-up dream for clarification can lead to one that helps interpret the earlier one. For example, before falling asleep, review the puzzling dream and think I desire a new dream to help me understand this one; or I desire a new dream with specifics on————. This is an important strategy if certain actions indicated by the dream are possible. It is best not to act hastily on dream material, especially if the information is general. A follow-on dream may provide details helpful for taking specific actions.

For example, your first dream may have alerted you to the possibility of locating helpful information for a project in some indistinct building. A follow-on dream might show the specific place—a certain bookstore or library. Perhaps a psi dream alerted you to a problem with someone, but the dream figure was indistinct. A follow-on dream could clarify who the individual is and permit you to plan accordingly.

With experience, psi dreams become easier to recognize. Our subconscious knows what is or is not of psi origin and it provides clues.

You may wake up simply knowing—or feeling—that you had a psi dream. It may have been presented in a different style from your ordinary dreams. Possibly it occurred just as you were drifting asleep or just waking up. It may not have seemed like a dream but like a remote viewing experience. Develop a strategy to help identify psi dreams. For example, desire them to have their message presented through a telephone call, on a television screen, or by some other means of communication. This does not mean all dreams with these or similar symbols are psi dreams. However, with practice, you will find that many are.

You may find that intending to recall only psi dreams on a specific night is a workable strategy for you. Most of your recalled dreams that night will likely be of psi origin. You may experience several dreams of the approaching situation or the psi target from different perspectives and with different aspects emphasized. By combining all the dreams, you can achieve a more complete understanding of the unknown situation or target.

A psi dream sometimes can be identified by the feelings it evokes. We simply know it was important. Sometimes the dream imagery has a different quality from that in ordinary dreams. Something about the dream compels us to give it more attention. Psi dreams usually have a simple message and are not as long as most personal dreams. Their pace may be faster. Sometimes a special emphasis in a psi dream will call attention to its psi origin—the scene may change abruptly or a spotlight could illuminate an object, for example. Occasionally psi information intrudes into an ordinary dream. Sudden shifts or out-of-context elements can alert us to that dream's psi aspects.

Psi dreams can follow ordinary dream dynamics. They usually have a beginning, middle, and end, like a well-told story. Usually the ending of a psi dream has the most relevant psi information, while the rest of the dream simply sets the stage for the emerging psi information.

With practice, you can learn to readily identify psi dreams from ordinary ones. In time, your dreaming mind can reliably show you a variety of psi or ESP phenomena, including clairvoyance, remote viewing, and telepathy. Psi dreams can include events from the past, those that are currently occurring, or future possibilities.

After psi Dreams

An important part of your psi dream process is recordkeeping. This is the key to tracking progress and understanding the nature of your psi dreams. The act of maintaining a detailed journal also reinforces your intent to have psi dreams. Writing about a psi dream helps the psi-dream process unfold. Giving your dream a title can also aid you in review activities.

Enter the details of your nightly dreams into a dedicated journal as soon as possible. Include as much detail as you can remember. If you recall many dreams, limit your writing to summaries or key phrases so that journal keeping does not become too time consuming.

Record in your journal a summary of your main activities and concerns from the previous day. This will help you sort ordinary personal or psychological dreams from potential psi dreams. For example, if you were sick or injured, a dream of an earthquake would very likely relate to your physical and mental situation, and not be a premonition. Note pressing physical or psychological situations. If you had a specific dream objective, be sure to record that intent clearly. This will help guide the understanding of any candidate psi dream that may have occurred. It is also important to identify any candidate psi dream or dream element for easy reference.

Preparing a summary of your suspected psi dreams in a separate journal will make it easier to retrieve for review. This summary could simply be a chronological list of dream titles such as "Debbie visits" and "Steve calls." Update your journal as soon as the suspected psi dream is confirmed and include all supporting information—what exactly happened, when, and where. Identify whom you had told about the dream before the dreamed-of incident occurred. If you missed identifying a psi-dream candidate and that incident later occurred, add that to your psi-dream summary, too.

If your psi-dream objective was to describe a place or thing that a friend had visited or observed, see if you can identify the target after recording all your dream impressions. Then, visit or observe that target for feedback. As we find with any learning task, this reinforces your intent and helps improve your psi processes. Feedback is invaluable for developing psi-dream proficiency, at least initially. New neurological pathways are formed in the brain that improve the efficiency of our links to regions involved in processing psi information. These pathways may also help in sorting psi impressions from other sources of mental activity such as imagination, memories, or interpretations. In addition, the physical act of doing something—visiting the site, looking at the picture—sends a strong affirming signal to your subconscious about your sincerity and desire to experience psi phenomena in the dream state.

When events you dreamed about occur, include the confirming information in your records. Note when the friend with whom you had lost touch called or what that newspaper headline showed. Attach photos or sketches of the event and note whether it was a spontaneous occurrence or in response to a focused intent or need.

For example, for those dream titles of "Debbie visits" or "Steve calls" you were alerted to the possibility of new, unexpected contact with Debbie or Steve. If you had no recent contact or dreams about them and they unexpectedly called you within a few days of the dream, you can consider those dreams to be examples of spontaneous psi experiences. Perhaps one or both of them had important information for you. However, had you been focusing on having a psi dream to alert you of unexpected incidents coming your way, then the dreams were responding to your intent.

As your recordkeeping progresses, look for emerging themes. Do your dreams follow any chronological pattern? Did you do better on certain kinds of needs or objectives? Are you better at dreaming scenes, people, or situations? How well do you pick up on feelings, moods, or emotions? What portion of the psi dream was symbolic and how much was literal? Working with visually dominant psi targets like real places, pictures, or objects is a good way to explore your psi-dream potential. For such targets, some people find their initial psi dreams only approximate the intended target. For example, a distant peak may be symbolized as a conical building in the dream. General shapes and forms are on track, but the specific target feature is not. With practice and perseverance, dream imagery can often, though not every time, more closely represent the intended target.

You also may want to estimate the accuracy of your psi dreams. Was the information sufficient to suggest a specific action to you? Did the psi dream have high, medium, or low correlation to ground truth? What factors, such as physical or mental well-being, may have affected the results?

It may be that not all suspected precognitive dreams come to pass, for which there are several reasons. The situation about which you dreamed may have been probable at the time of the dream, but something unforeseen has since occurred, which changed the flow of events. Perhaps a sudden change of plans caused your friend to cancel or postpone the call or trip.

This would also be explained if the suspected psi dream actually was, instead, one of the personal type. In that case, reexamine it from a personal perspective. Maybe you misinterpreted it or the time frame is too far in the future. Initially, you may want to focus on precognitive psi dreams for a predetermined time only—perhaps no more than one week ahead—but, as you gain experience, be open to extending the horizon to longer time periods.

You will want to record what actions you took when you received dreams of a warning nature. To what extent could you avoid the approaching situation or alert others to it? Research on spontaneous precognitive experiences of a personal nature indicate that we can take actions to avoid unpleasant situations. Even if you could not take action, the dream may have occurred for a purpose, if only to affirm your psi-dream potential. Maybe you had a former link with the area about which you dreamed; perhaps you have a strong interest in or concern about a certain topic, which the dream helped fulfill.

If precognitive psi dreams alerted you to approaching opportunities, to what extent were you better prepared to accept them as a result of having had the dream? If it provided information you needed, how did you integrate that into your daily life? Precognitive dreams usually depict what is potential, not necessarily what is fixed. We still need to strive for achieving the potential future, if they are situations in line with our goals.

Be sure your responses to any dream are of a constructive nature. It is vital that you exercise good judgment and caution if, based on your psi dream, particular actions can be taken. For example, say your psi dream relates to an approaching situation that will affect someone else. Be sure to use tact and good sense in determining how to present this information to that person. Our dreaming mind is there to help us and others, not impede us or cause distress in any way. Dreams can overdramatize a situation. We must be cautious, especially if actions we take involve other people.

As You Progress

As you gain confidence, psi dreaming becomes easier.

You may want to focus only on psi dreams that are of immediate help, such as those that alert you to approaching incidents or those that assist in finding missing people or objects. You may want to develop a comprehensive way of exploring psi dreams by working with others, who can prepare a variety of targets and serve as observers or beacon persons. Systematic approaches for psi dreaming and keeping track of progress can be similar to those used for doing remote viewing.

As you open up your psi-dream capabilities, other aspects of your life will improve. You will gain a better understanding of the viewpoints and feelings of others. Your levels and uses of intuition and creativity will improve, and you will experience more frequent events demonstrating synchronicity. Working with psi dreams also improves your talents in other psi activities such as remote viewing.

As long as you remain open to having psi dreams and are willing to record their details and consider their implications, you will continue to have them. In time, you will find a psi-dream pace that is appropriate for you. When psi dreaming becomes second nature, you will benefit from them routinely.

Psi dreaming can let us discover the far reaches of our mind and take us on an exciting journey of inner exploration.

21
Seeking
Synchronicities

The causality principle asserts that the connection between cause and effect is a necessary one.

The synchronicity principle asserts that the terms of a meaningful coincidence are connected by simultaneity and meaning.

—Carl Jung, *Synchronicity: An Acausal Connecting Principle* (page 69)

WE ARE CONSCIOUSLY AND UNCONSCIOUSLY ON THE ALERT FOR MEANINGFUL information, which may come to us through our senses, subliminal impressions, or our psi nature. Something important may be found at a specific location, or it may be known to a certain individual—all we need to do is locate it or make contact.

Within practical constraints, we can sometimes take an active role in discovering something significant at the appropriate time. We need to be open to hunches and intuitions that nudge our path toward the source of that help. When we make such discoveries, we can consider the incident to be a subconsciously assisted event or a meaningful coincidence. This is called "synchronicity."

Sometimes the paths of others are gently pushed into a timely meeting or meaningful intersection with our own. When this happens, the other person's psi nature has detected our concerns and has prompted them with intuitions and hunches that led to that need-fulfilling event. Although synchronicities may occur infrequently if unbidden, it is possible to experience them more often when we desire to do so.

Some synchronicities result from a subconscious need. They may occur in order to call our attention to certain patterns, an unsuspected insight, or to encourage us to follow new learning paths. In such instances, we may be responding to our deeper nature and transpersonal connectivities. Synchronicities of this type help us become aware that there is more to our nature than the surface levels of conscious awareness. We begin to look beyond our ego and to become open to aspects of ourselves that we may have been ignoring. We discover new channels of creativity. They have significance beyond any apparent need and may have various levels of meaning. They resemble the functioning of holograms: by connecting patterns that help bring about a greater whole in a trend toward fulfillment and unity.

We have a tendency to search for patterns and to seek their meaning. When we discover that something that resonates with us has meaning, we may not understand why it has this effect on us. Somehow we feel it to be true and we gain new motivation or a new sense of purpose from that incident. Our search for patterns and for that sense of resonance suggests that our psyche has features similar to a hologram's.

In physics, a hologram occurs when electromagnetic waves—light, radio—or other types of waves—acoustic, water—interact to form patterns. Usually laser light is used to create a hologram, since the frequencies are coherent, or in phase. To create a hologram, laser light illuminates objects—say a chair and an apple. Another portion of that light is recombined with the light reflected from the chair and apple, recorded on film—the hologram—and developed. At that point all that can be seen is something that looks like many fingerprints in complex patterns of light areas and dark lines. When the same laser light illuminates that film, however, a three-dimensional image of the chair and apple appear to pop out of the film, appearing as real objects.

If laser light is reflected off the chair when the apple is absent, then passed through the hologram, only a three-dimensional image of the apple will appear. The chair, when illuminated, brings the other part of the original pattern, which contains the apple, back to view. The chair has resonated with the apple that is embedded, or enfolded, in the hologram. The hologram can be cut into tiny pieces and the apple and the chair can be made visible from any one of the small sections, though not as accurately as they would be from the original hologram.

In a similar way, our subconscious mind may at times resonate with hidden patterns deep in our psyche. Seeing or experiencing something that belongs to that pattern may be the trigger for that *Aha!* feeling, that sudden impulse. We may only dimly be aware of the meaning of that pattern, but somehow we are drawn to pursue it and complete the essence of the hidden picture. A feeling of wholeness is invoked by our resonance with that pattern.

Synchronistic events toss hints of how our subconscious mind may operate and suggest that aspects of our brain and deep layers of our psyche may be wavelike in nature, similar to the manner in which a hologram functions.

Experiencing Synchronicities

To experience synchronicities and increase the frequency of their occurrence:

- ➤ Accept the reality of synchronistic events.
- ➤ Maintain a strong focus on a specific need.
- ➤ Accomplish whatever you can to achieve that need through ordinary means.
- ➤ Hold strong intent on experiencing a synchronicity to provide assistance.
- ➤ Be flexible and open to receiving intuitions and hunches.

Although you may occasionally experience synchronicities, you can expect them more frequently by simply accepting their reality. Assume that you can experience them, then anticipate their occurrence. You have the potential to experience synchronicity whenever you have a pressing need or concern. As you strive to resolve that need, you will automatically devote considerable mental energy to that issue. You will become singly focused. As you do everything you can through ordinary means, you affirm to your subconscious mind the importance of that need. The intensity of physical and mental effort sets the stage for psi assistance through synchronistic events when they are feasible.

Some individuals report increases in synchronicity as a result of the mental discipline that is called upon for yoga or meditation practices. Such practices make us more receptive to subconscious activity, which opens us to our intuitive and psychic nature as well as to our synchronistic connections. Consistent meditation practice that promotes feelings of unity or oneness with others and the environment helps promote synchronistic occurrences for some people. Others arrive at similar effects when they become absorbed in a creative activity, walk in a natural area, or read poetry or other material that helps them reach beyond the surface ego.

As you accomplish whatever you can to resolve a specific need, keep the possibility of synchronistic assistance in mind. Set aside time for intentionally seeking synchronistic help. For example, during relaxation or meditation, occasionally think: I desire a synchronicity for helping to ———. Be specific. Mention the exact need or issue, keep this thought firmly in mind, then let it go. Intend it to be a sincere message or request to your subconscious for consideration and action. As in any creative or psi activity, we cannot insist or force the issue; that brings our surface ego into the foreground and can short-circuit our subtle subconscious processes.

The key is the repeated utterance of the simple request: "I desire a synchronistic experience for helping to ———." Then relax and remain quiet. Keep all other thoughts to a minimum. If you begin thinking about routine matters, chase those thoughts away. Focus on your breathing until you again reach a quiet, calm state. Then occasionally repeat your intent for synchronistic help. Do this frequently during the day, for several minutes each time. You may do this during a routine task, while engaged in mild physical activity such as walking, or at any convenient time. Before you fall asleep at night repeat this request.

Then expect the unexpected. Days or weeks may pass. Synchronicities involve a subconscious process that cannot be forced. Even if nothing synchronistic occurs, don't be discouraged. There may be practical reasons why synchronistic help could not be available at that time. Simply continue with your requests. Perhaps you will be drawn to a place you do not usually visit and find the help you need. On impulse, you may visit a library at just the time a helpful book is returned. You may be attracted toward an individual who can give assistance. In some situations you need to do very little. A friend who can help you may suddenly have the urge to call or send a letter. Someone you routinely associate with may supply aid unexpectedly.

You can assist the synchronistic process by being flexible. Break away from routine habits. Be open and spontaneous. This availability increases your associations with others. The more interactions you have, the more likely your subconscious processes are to bring you into meaningful intersections and experience synchronicities. Simply by being spontaneous and alert, synchronicities will increase. Maybe subliminal sensitivities will lead to some of them or maybe your psi nature will be totally responsible, but it does not matter how you receive synchronistic help. Something unusual occurred—simply accept it.

At times we may come close to experiencing synchronicity but fail to recognize it or link it up, especially if the necessary paths move quickly and the window of opportunity is brief. Being in the right place at the right time may not be enough. You still need help connecting with the person who can help by initiating conversation. You may need to look harder for that important book or missing item. Certainly your hunches and intuitions become guides, but you need to be open and receptive to them.

As you experience synchronicities, your belief in and acceptance of them increases and you encounter them more frequently. Not all may relate to a pressing need. Sometimes they result from our curiosity about something. They may lead to humorous or creative incidents and give us new ideas that aren't directly associated with our immediate concerns. At such times, our subconscious needs may have surfaced.

Recognizing Synchronicities

Usually it is easy to recognize when we have a synchronistic experience. Something unexpected occurs that is directly related to a pressing issue or concern at the time we need that help. The combination of need and timing rules out simple chance as an explanation for most, if not all, of them. We experience many coincidences but they usually have no relevance to our current needs. The test is need and timing: Did the event provide help at the time you needed it?

We can sense when an event is synchronistic in other ways as well. A dream may alert us to an approaching incident that proves to be synchronistic. We then can recognize this dream to have been of psi origin. This illustrates how our subconscious mind sensed the possibility of an emerging synchronicity. We may feel or sense a growing excitement that then may result in a sudden urge to do something unusual.

Some people can tell an event is synchronistic from their subjective reaction to it. The experience feels uniquely different from a chance encounter. Sometimes such experiences are accompanied by a feeling of déjà vu. The strangely familiar event seems as if we had somehow known that it would occur and how it would play out once it did take place.

Synchronistic experiences can lead us to suspect that something exceptional has been made available. They can invoke a variety of feelings—a sense of awe, delightful surprise, humility, or even humor, which can be a way of dealing with the uncanny feelings that the occurrence of dramatic synchronicities can evoke. Whatever our reaction, we somehow know that a subconscious process that connects us with others or with our environment has been revealed to us.

As You Proceed

After a synchronistic experience, you may wish to acknowledge quietly your appreciation to your subconscious creative process for the extra help you received. This act conveys your interest in synchronicity and helps facilitate their future occurrence. Of course, whatever information, insight, or motivation the experience provided should be applied in resolving the specific need that led to the event.

As you would when practicing remote viewing or psi dreamwork, you should keep good records. Simply writing out the incident reinforces your sincerity about synchronicities and helps encourage their reoccurrence for future needs. Your records will prove to be valuable for yourself and others. Use them to relive the experience when you need inspiration or confidence. Other people seeking synchronistic experiences can gain insight and confidence from your records as well. Good records allow you to detect patterns in your synchronistic experiences. Under what conditions did they occur? How frequently did they arise? How important were the needs?

A detailed journal can also assist you in discovering links between synchronistic events and intuitions, psi dreams, and other forms of psi perception. Simply writing about synchronicities stimulates creative ideas and new interests. You will sense more of your own deeper nature as well as the ways in which we all are interconnected. As you experience increased synchronicities for receiving help, you may also find yourself drawn into situations that are helpful for others. You will become involved in helping them experience their own synchronicity. A sudden impulse may motivate you to call or write to someone and give them help they had not expected. You may find yourself in the right place at the right time to assist them at a time of need.

After you have experienced your initial synchronicities and have established good recordkeeping, occasionally hold the intent for experiencing them. The issues do not need to be critical. Synchronicities occur equally for great and small situations. Simply affirm your desire to be open and receptive to them, maintain a spontaneous flexible style, and look forward to another adventure. Let your intuition guide the way.

Synchronicities do not occur in isolation from other subconscious processes. As you experience them more frequently, you can expect your intuition and dream recall to increase as well. Other psi experiences—remote viewing, telepathy, precognition—also can occur more easily and frequently. Synchronistic experiences can motivate new creative activities. Being open to synchronicities improves your sense of connectivity. You can live more efficiently and effectively and have the potential for helping others at times when no other means is apparent.

For many of us, the most exciting and rewarding experiences that we can have during our much-too-short lifetime are those springing from within. Life can be—should be—a journey of discovery. As we explore the nature of our own being, we can come to know more about that deeper and truer essence within ourselves and others. We uncover more of our innate creativity. We open up our intuition. We bring forth our psi nature. We can then be more at ease, or at one, with ourselves, others, and our environment. As we explore, we discover trails with many intersections. Some are marked "Synchronicity." Sometimes those trails have clear tracks we can follow. At other times we glimpse only faint traces that point deeper into an unknown wilderness. Yet something calls us to follow, to explore ahead.

Anyone can seek those tracks and make surprising discoveries. *Tracks in the psychic wilderness* can be found.

Afterword

THE WILDERNESS TRAILS I HAVE EXPLORED HAD MARKERS LEFT BY THOSE SEARCHERS who followed these paths before me. Now, other explorers enter the forest at different points and head in different directions following signs that are familiar to them. These markers—and our words for them—help guide us and keep us afloat. Sometimes we feel we are in a dark forest or traveling over seas of darkness. To quote Goethe: "When the mind is at sea, a new word provides a raft."

I have tracked psi and other inhabitants of our inner domain employing the language and the signposts that are familiar to me as an experimental scientist as well as the intuition I have developed as a wilderness tracker. I continue to look for new markers, new tracks. Occasionally I glimpse others on nearby trails. I look forward to many interesting intersections on the trails ahead.

Appendix

Concepts and Projections

A recent observation from Bell's Theorem in quantum physics demonstrates that certain properties of elementary particles that originally coupled can remain correlated even when the particles have become separated by great distance. This correlation between their spin, or similar property, occurs instantaneously with no known law of cause and effect and is called quantum synchronicity. In essence, a meaningful connection continues to exist between the particles in some type of holistic and nonlocal relationship. This effect suggests that elementary matter has undiscovered connecting principles. Such correlations lend support to the fundamental ordering principle that physicist David Bohm termed the "implicate order."

The activity or motion of this hidden pattern, the holomovement, leads to surface movements, an explicit order, in our space-time world. This invokes the idea of a scintillating hologram, which is formed by wave-interference patterns. All information within the entire hologram is also contained in any portion of the hologram, no matter how small. A hologram represents space-time information in the form of patterns and relationships. The original spatial information can be reconstructed by illuminating the hologram with the original wave, usually laser light. Certain brain activities are wavelike and suggest a holographic essence, such as how some forms of memory or recognition may result from wavelike electrical patterns and their interactions. The discovery of microtubules—unusual cylindrical structures—in the brain may have implications for quantum processes. These structures are of a size suitable for sustaining stable, or coherent, quantum effects. If this is the case, these structures may have a role in how psi information is initially perceived.

In Bohm's view, matter emerges from the underlying holomovement as stationary or dynamic patterns of wave interactions. Relationships among objects are more important than the individual objects' separate identities. This is a departure from Einstein's view of the universe, in which matter results from a stable but elastic configuration of the space-time continuum.

Measurements in quantum physics recognize an observer effect: the nature of what is measured depends on how the measurement—the inter-action—is constructed. Participation in the measurement event affects the outcome. Thus, the observer is part of the interaction process; a particle can be observed either as a wave, or as a particle. Similarly, a wave, includ-ing light, can be observed as a particle or as a wave, but not as both at the same time.

Rupert Sheldrake, a British biochemist, proposed the concept of a uni-versal morphogenic field, a type of holistic field or force that is fundamental to how living organisms develop. Sheldrake suspects that morphogenic fields influence patterns of brain activity associated with behavior through some type of resonance. Once a behavior or certain thought patterns occur, they are easier for any member of that species to reproduce. There is a similarity between Sheldrake's morphic fields and the archetypes—uni-versal patterns in the psyche—proposed by C. G. Jung, a pioneer in dream-work and consciousness studies.

The informational aspects of psi—ESP, remote viewing, precognition—man-ifest best as patterns or portions of a pattern, suggesting that psi has a holographic nature. Consciousness, therefore, must also have, or be able to interact with, this holographic essence.

Psi phenomena can be considered as a means or as a process. Con-sciousness interacts with this process at two levels: (1) perceiving, and (2) knowing or giving meaning. In the future, a new field of quantum physics that considers the role of consciousness may emerge. This field would examine psi phenomena and the interface between the physical and the mental natures of ourselves and the universe. The essence of this "quan-tum consciousness" will probably have a wavelike and nonlocal nature.

Quantum consciousness will probably incorporate an observable ele-ment of human personality, feeling, and intellect (meaning) into its basic parameters. It may be that a consciousness field (and its wavelike attributes) will eventually be seen as a multidimensional extension of the existing space-time continuum.

Successful informational psi experiments at global distances show that psi can reach across space in ways similar to nonlocal quantum effects. Psi experiments in which individuals focus intent on influencing instruments, such as electronic devices, have also been successful at long distances. The devices generate a series of random data bits, similar to computer off–on signals. These electronic "coin flippers" make it easy to study possible interactions resulting from conscious intent while someone focuses on influencing the events one way (more 0s) or the other (more 1s). Although effects are small, over time they accumulate to statistical significance.

A variation of this focused-direction approach is simply to keep attention on the device, then examine the degree of order (less variability) in the random data stream. If consciousness has quantumlike properties, it should then be able to inject order into a random system simply by observation. Consciousness and unconsciousness appear to have an aspect that is order driven and seeks higher levels of coherence, such as we observe in evolution. When such experiments of focused attention are carried out, the results show that the degree of order or balance has in fact improved to statistical levels of significance.

Another way of looking at this is to consider mental intent as affecting an existing consciousness/subconsciousness field—something like the way the moon affects gravity and tide levels. As mental intent becomes focused through concentration or heightened emotional levels, the entire consciousness field responds in some way. Some people are naturally more sensitive to such effects than others. It is as if they sensed a signal propagating through the consciousness field at large. Detectors that have some quantum properties should also be influenced by that disturbance or signal. That is exactly what experiments with random-event generators indicate. In the case of random-event generators, the effect of this signal is to smooth out the inherent randomness. However, the meaning or significance of the effect cannot be deduced—only another sensitive mind can do that.

Similar results are observed when such a random event–generating device is in the presence of a group of people who become highly focused on an event. They do not need to focus on the device, or even know of its existence. Experiments have been carried out during high emotional television programs seen by a large audience, such as the Academy Award ceremonies or the announcement of the verdict at the O. J. Simpson trial. The devices showed that an increase in order over baseline measurements occurred, supporting the existence of a consciousness-field effect. Correlations occurred between device behavior and times of highly emotional situations. Additional experiments of the type are discussed in Dean Radin's *The Conscious Universe*.

Montague Ullman, a pioneer in dream research, has proposed that dream states are particularly conducive to experiencing not only personal dreams, but also dreams relating to overall trends in society's development and to its emerging needs. Through dreams and intuitions, some individuals are driven to pursue certain activities in such areas as politics, art, or science, at great personal risk. To them, the overall benefit to society from these efforts is more important than personal risk and their own self-protection. Such urgings may have their origin in some higher-order evolutionary tendency derived from a global consciousness- (or subconscious-) field effect. The idea of a consciousness field is not new. This is similar to Jung's collective unconscious and the morphogenic field posited by Sheldrake.

Psi research has demonstrated that people can sense when someone else is focusing attention on them, even though there is no conscious awareness of that intent. Experiments in which physiological parameters such as skin electrical (electrodermal) conductivity are measured show correlations to times when a distant person is focusing attention on that person. Although the effects are small, they can be verified by statistical methods.

Several hundred studies of this type have been performed, and they confirm that our brain has the capability of detecting another person's intention, even though we remain consciously unaware of that intent. Thus, under some circumstances, it may be possible for people to mentally influence someone's immune system in beneficial ways in order to assist them in recovery from illness or accident. Distant healing, therefore, can have a potential use as an adjunct to conventional recovery practices. Other studies have examined effects of mental intention on cells and other biological systems. Correlations between mental intention and an examined parameter—cell-growth rate, for example—have been observed.

The nonlocal coupling of distant particles points toward a hidden unifying principle independent of time or distance. Bohm's holomovement, Sheldrake's morphic field, and the observer effect in quantum physics all provide concepts for building toward a model of mind-matter connectivity. This could lead to recognition, and possibly understanding, of psi phenomena and synchronistic experiences.

There is a growing public awareness that our mind has both a logical and a nonlogical, intuitive nature that works best when they are in balance. As we understand more about the nature of consciousness, we discover more about the nature of psi. This evolution of understanding—and acceptance—will make it easier for others to explore psi openly, especially younger people who are not as strongly bound to cultural beliefs or expectations as their parents. Regardless of theories about psi, or how it can manifest, the pursuit of psi applications will continue as it always has. If it works, then use it. There are no useless phenomena in the universe. As psi applications expand, psi will become an integrated and balanced part of society's evolution.

As more people become open to psi, not only will the psychological setting change, but so will the coherence of the consciousness field at large. It will become easier to attune to that subconscious evolutionary tendency toward order and unity. As with breaking the four-minute mile, once the breakthrough occurs, others more easily accomplish what had previously been accepted to be an impossible feat. Our collective unconscious seems to be very adaptable and may, in fact, also evolve to reflect specific needs and achievements. Like a muscle, the more we exercise it, the more we not only improve our own mental and physical responses, but also add that achievement to the consciousness field at large. Others can then benefit, no matter where they are.

There will be at least three groups who will develop a psi acceptance:

(1) those who simply want to apply psi, if only occasionally, for help in some way in their own lives; (2) those who are motivated to use psi for helping others; and (3) scientists, theologians, philosophers, and others interested in developing or expanding theories on how the universe operates and the nature of our role in it.

As the possibility of psi, and psi-research and application results, become better known, a lifting of the psi barrier will occur. There will still be those who will resist. However, the rationale for their resistance will become less persuasive in view of the growing evidence for psi. Furthermore, more people will take a look for themselves. No one needs an expert to verify it. Anyone can search for truth themselves. In fact, most people already rely on some form of intuition, or have an occasional gut feeling that proves to be true. In the future, more people will experience psi frequently.

As people who pursue psi eventually find out, they will not want to keep it all to themselves. Something in us, a type of creative urge, wants us to share talents. More people will find ways to apply psi for helping others. Intuitive diagnostics, police casework, archaeological projects, and search-and-rescue missions are some of the possibilities. The growing realization of psi's effectiveness at a distance will also generate new interest in mental healing, which will become the most widely applied form of psi phenomena.

As more scientists and others come to examine the implications of psi and quantum consciousness, the more diverse scientific-integrating activity will become. New understanding of our nature and our role in the universe will emerge and new questions will arise. For example, to what extent does group negativity (e.g., those focused on destruction) influence the subconscious activity of others, even at great distances? Similarly, to what extent would group harmony and a focus on positive thoughts influence potential undesirable actions in others? What are the implications for evolution? For the usually unspoken search for meaning?

In the immediate future, it seems reasonable to set up an international consortium that would examine practical applications of psi at a global level. At first, only select projects would be considered, such as searches for missing people, prediction of terrorist acts, or the pursuit of psi communication for joint American-Russian space projects. Such activities would, of course, have to be well planned to avoid difficulties that usually accompany new joint ventures. This group would work closely with the Parapsychological Association, the existing international psi research group. In time, the practical utility of psi, when approached carefully and kept in perspective, will receive wide acceptance. When prodded by public mandate, governments and private enterprise will endorse, if not support, activities for evaluating and locating individuals with highly repeatable psi proficiency similar to current searches for achievers in mathematics or science. Databases will be developed for individual track records and to facilitate personal selection for national and global projects.

As international awareness of psi and its potential use grows, the prospects of international psi applications increase. Sometime in the next century the perception of Louisa Rhine will become a reality. In *Hidden Channel of the Mind*, she writes: "If precognitive ability is developed and directed, as in time it is reasonable to expect it will be, its operation, even on a limited basis, could obviously be of untold value to humanity" (page 189).

Currently, many people are opening up to their intuitive and psi nature. Anyone can become part of this growing trend, to help themselves and others, and to make a difference in the world we live in.

As we approach the arbitrary milestone of the year 2000, it is convenient to muse on what the past one hundred years have shown us about ourselves and the universe. The twentieth century has been truly amazing. Think how much more amazement is yet to be discovered in the century ahead.

Resources

Books

Bohm, David. *Wholeness and the Implicate Order.* London: Routledge & Kegan Paul, 1983.

Bosnak, Robert. *Tracks in the Wilderness of Dreaming.* New York: Delacorte Press, 1996.

Broughton, Richard. *Parapsychology: The Controversial Science.* New York: Ballantine, 1991.

Czetli, Steve, and Nancy Myer-Czetli. *Silent Witness.* New York: Birch Lane Press, 1993.

Delaney, Gale. *New Directions in Dream Interpretation.* Albany: State of New York Press, 1995.

Garfield, Patricia. *Creative Dreaming.* New York: Ballantine, 1974.

Jahn, Robert, and Brenda Dunne. *Margins of Reality: The Role of Consciousness in the Physical World.* San Diego, Calif.: Harcourt Brace, 1987.

Jung, Carl G. *Synchronicity: An Acausal Connecting Principle.* Princeton, N.J.: Princeton University Press, 1973.

Krippner, Stanley, and Joseph Dillard. *Dreamworking.* Buffalo, N.Y.: Bearly Limited, 1988.

LaBerge, Stephen. *Exploring the World of Lucid Dreams.* New York: Ballantine, 1990.

McMoneagle, Joseph. *Mind Trek.* Charlottesville, Va.: Hampton Roads, 1993.

Mishlove, Jeffrey. *PSI Development Systems.* New York: Ballantine, 1988.

Mitchell, Edgar. *Psychic Exploration: A Challenge for Science.* John White, ed. New York: G. P. Putman's Sons; 1974.

———. *The Way of the Explorer.* New York: Putnam, 1996.

Orloff, Judith. *Second Sight.* New York: Warner, 1996.

Puthoff, Harold, and Russell Targ. *Mind Reach.* New York: Delacorte Press, 1977.

Radin, Dean. *The Conscious Universe.* San Francisco: HarperCollins, 1997.

Rhine, Louisa E. *ESP in Life and Lab.* Toronto: Collier Macmillan, 1967.

———. *The Invisible Picture: A Study of Psychic Experiences.* Jefferson, N.C.: McFarland, 1981.

Sheldrake, Robert. *A New Science of Life.* London: Blond and Briggs, 1981.

Sherman, Harold, and Hubert Wilkins. *Thoughts Through Space*. Amherst, Wisc.: Amherst Press, 1983.

Stiffler, LaVonne. *Synchronicity and Reunion: The Genetic Connection to Adoptees and Birthparents*. Hobe Sound, Fla.: FEA Publishing, 1992.

Talbot, Michael. *The Holographic Universe*. New York: HarperCollins, 1991.

Ullman, Montague, Stanley Krippner, and Alan Vaughan. *Dream Telepathy*. New York: Penguin, 1974.

Ullman, Montague, and Nan Zimmerman. *Working with Dreams*. New York: Delacorte, 1979.

Internet Resources

Baycliff psi Seminars
➤ http://www.chesapeake.net/~baygraff/

Consciousness Research Laboratory
➤ http://www.psiresearch.org

Cognitive Sciences Laboratory
➤ http://www.jsasoc.com/csl/index.html/

Exceptional Human Experience Network, Inc
➤ http://www.ehe.edu

Koestler Parapsychology Unit
➤ http://www.moebius.psy.ed.ac.uk/index.html

Intuition Network
➤ http://www.Intuition.org

Parapsychology Links
➤ http://www.mdani.demon.co.uk/para/paralink.htm